DEE VALLEY, CLWYDIAN HILLS AND NORTH EAST WALES

Outstanding Circular Walks

Compiled by Terry Marsh

Contents

At-a-glance	2	Short walks up to 2½ hours	11
Keymap	4	Slightly harder walks of 2½–3½ hours	46
Introduction	6	Longer walks of 4 hours and over	67
		Further Information	92

At-a-glance

Walk		Page	Start	Grid ref	Distance	Ascent	Time
1	Coed y Gopa	12	Abergele (south)	SH 933 771	2 miles (3km)	690ft (210m)	1¼ hrs
2	Valle Crucis Abbey	14	Horseshoe Falls car park	SJ 197 433	2½ miles (4km)	460ft (140m)	1½ hrs
3	Greenfield Valley Heritage Park	16	Greenfield	SJ 196 775	3 miles (5km)	525ft (160m)	1¾ hrs
4	Northop	19	Northop	SJ 245 683	3 miles (5km)	195ft (60m)	1¾ hrs
5	St Asaph and Afon Elwy	22	St Asaph	SJ 036 743	3 miles (5km)	215ft (65m)	1¾ hrs
6	Great Orme	24	Great Orme Country Park	SH 765 833	3¼ miles (5.25km)	625ft (190m)	2 hrs
7	Castell Dinas Bran	26	Llangollen	SJ 217 421	3 miles (5km)	855ft (260m)	2 hrs
8	Llannefydd and Mynydd y Gaer	28	Llannefydd	SH 981 706	3½ miles (5.6km)	690ft (210m)	2 hrs
9	Caergwrle and Hope	30	Caergwrle	SJ 305 574	3¾ miles (6km)	375ft (115m)	2 hrs
10	Denbigh and the Ystrad valley	32	Denbigh town centre	SJ 050 661	5 miles (8km)	575ft (175m)	2½ hrs
11	A taste of the Llangollen Canal	35	Llangollen	SJ 217 421	4½ miles (7km)	260ft (80m)	2½ hrs
12	Hawarden	38	Hawarden	SJ 315 656	4½ miles (7km)	460ft (140m)	2½ hrs
13	Dyserth and Graig Fawr	40	Dyserth	SJ 062 792	4½ miles (7km)	560ft (170m)	2½ hrs
14	Along the River Clwyd	42	Rhyl, Marine Lake	SH 996 806	5½ miles (9km)	70ft (20m)	2½ hrs
15	Cyrn-y-brain	44	Ponderosa Café	SJ 192 481	4¼ miles (7km)	590ft (180m)	2½ hrs
16	Tremeirchion	47	Tremeirchion	SJ 081 726	5 miles (8km)	935ft (285m)	2¾ hrs
17	Ty Mawr and Pontcysyllte Aqueduct	50	Ty Mawr Country Park	SJ 283 414	5½ miles (9km)	500ft (150m)	2¾ hrs
18	Prestatyn Hillside	53	Prestatyn	SJ 074 819	5¼ miles (8.3km)	760ft (230m)	2¾ hrs
19	Llandegla and Moel y Waun	56	Llandegla	SJ 196 523	5½ miles (8.7km)	705ft (215m)	3 hrs
20	Chirk and the River Ceiriog	59	Chirk	SJ 291 376	5¾ miles (9.2km)	975ft (295m)	3 hrs
21	Moel Famau	62	Moel Famau Country Park	SJ 172 611	5¼ miles (8.25km)	1,265ft (385m)	3 hrs
22	Loggerheads and Cilcain	64	Loggerheads Country Park	SJ 197 626	6½ miles (10.5km)	890ft (270m)	3 hrs
23	Penycloddiau and Moel Arthur	68	Llangwyfan	SJ 139 667	7½ miles (12km)	1,675ft (510m)	4¼ hrs
24	Llantysilio Mountain	72	Ponderosa Café	SJ 192 481	7½ miles (12km)	1,855ft (565m)	4½ hrs
25	Llyn Brenig	76	Llyn Brenig visitor centre	SH 967 546	9 miles (14.5km)	950ft (290m)	4½ hrs
26	Point of Ayr and the Wales Coast Path	80	Point of Ayr	SJ 124 847	9 miles (14.5km)	215ft (65m)	4 hrs
27	Bwlch Maen Gwynedd and Cadair Bronwen	84	Llandrillo	SJ 035 371	8½ miles (13.6km)	2,265ft (690m)	5 hrs
28	Moel Sych and Cadair Berwyn	88	Milltir Cerrig	SJ 017 305	8½ miles (13.5km)	1,295ft (395m)	5 hrs

Comments

A relaxing exploration of a glorious Woodland Trust property including an Iron Age hillfort, bountiful wildlife and extensive views over the coastlands of North Wales.

An easy walk leads initially through birch woodland to an ancient abbey, before descending to the Llangollen Canal and spending time between canal and river.

A delightful stroll through a lush valley that has seen extensive industry in the past, a long monastic presence and has an abundance of wildlife.

A relaxing walk from the appealing and ancient village of Northop, through the grounds of the ancient country house of Soughton Hall. Part of the walk follows the course of an ancient earthwork, Wat's Dyke.

An easy walk from the historic city of St Asaph into the farming countryside to the north, completed by a return along the Afon Elwy.

There are impressive views of Llandudno, along the coast and across the Conwy estuary to the mountains of Snowdonia on this short circuit of the Great Orme.

Too good to ignore, the steady climb to the summit of Dinas Bran is eased by zigzags and wide-ranging views over the green Denbighshire landscapes.

A moderately-easy walk from the pleasant village of Llannefydd to a prehistoric hillfort with far-reaching views across the Clwydian Hills and into Snowdonia (Eryri).

As well as Hope Mountain, there are distant views of the Dee estuary on this undemanding walk in the valley of the River Alyn.

Pleasant walking in the valley of the Afon Ystrad is followed by great views of Denbigh Castle across the Vale of Clwyd.

A straightforward stroll along the Llangollen Canal to reach the magnificent Pontcysyllte Aqueduct.

A pleasant easy-moderate walk through the woodlands, parklands and estate of Hawarden Castle. Many stiles are encountered en route along with fine views of the Flintshire countryside.

A visit to the Woodland Trust lands of Graig Fawr and a taste of Offa's Dyke Path make for an interesting tour to the north-east of Dyserth.

A simple and straightforward amble along both sides of the Afon Clwyd, linking the coastal resort of Rhyl with inland Rhuddlan; plenty of scope for observing birdlife along the way.

A straightforward out and back walk to a Marilyn summit with extensive views of the Clwydian Hills and much of Wales, and a Bronze Age cairn.

An undulating ramble among the foothills of the Clwydians that rises to the Offa's Dyke Path and the summit of Cefn Du before easing down to the Vale of Clwyd.

The dominating feature of this walk is Telford's majestic Pontcysyllte Aqueduct, which carries the Shropshire Union Canal over the Dee valley.

From this northerly section of the Clwydian mountain range, the views are splendid, extending over Prestatyn and Rhyl and along the coast to Llandudno and the Great Orme.

A most agreeable walk along a stretch of Offa's Dyke Path rising to a fine viewpoint, and followed by quiet lanes flanked by a wide variety of wildflowers.

A walk through the parkland of Chirk castle is followed by a dramatic descent into the lovely Ceiriog valley. Towards the end you pass beneath an adjacent viaduct and then an aqueduct.

This approach to Moel Famau is circuitous, starting to the south and following 'The Mushroom Path'. Eventually, the route joins Offa's Dyke Path to the summit of the hill before a descent through woodland.

An easy but rambling circular walk starting from the popular Loggerheads Country Park and then following in the footsteps of Felix Mendelssohn, the German composer.

With such far-reaching views, it's easy to see why the Clwydian Hills were favoured for the route of Offa's Dyke; this walk follows well-defined tracks and visits two Iron Age hillforts.

A splendid up and down route, often steep, across heathery uplands leads to a more relaxed return above the valley of the Afon Morwynion.

This lengthy but easy circuit of Llyn Brenig romps across heathland and through part of the Clocaenog Forest, with extensive views of the heather moorlands of Mynydd Hiraethog.

A linear walk that for much of the way favours the coastal sand dunes before joining the seafront at Prestatyn. A chance to get a taste of the Wales Coast Path – and ice cream!

Taking you high onto the summit ridge of the Berwyn Mountains, the half way point, from which Cadair Bronwen can be achieved, is a distinct pass crossing the ridge. Cadair Bronwen is linked in legend with King Arthur.

An uncomplicated route across heather moorland, much on boardwalks, to the twin high points of the Berwyn Range. There are extensive views that embrace almost the whole of Wales.

Keymap

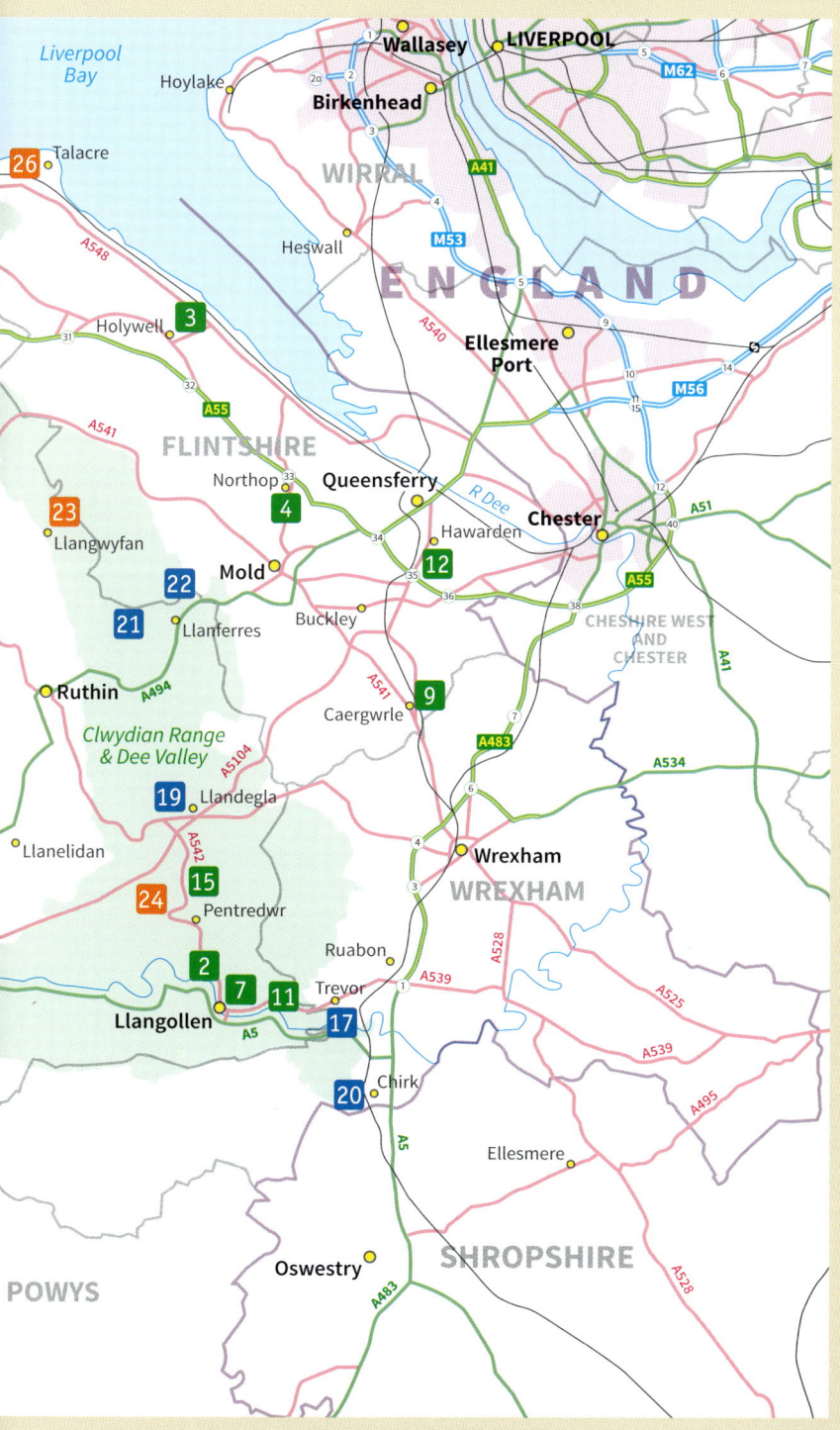

Introduction to the Dee Valley, Clwydian Hills and North East Wales

This title covers North East Wales roughly east of the Conwy valley and from Bala Lake up to the Dee estuary and embraces the Clwydian Hills and the Vale of Clwyd, extending south-west of Llangollen into the Berwyn Hills for good measure. All the walks serve to demonstrate what a delectable part of Wales this north-easterly corner is, with walks to suit all tastes from linear tramps through coastal sand dunes to breezy summits, religious sites, and valleys heady with the tang of the country's past.

To get the most out of the area, it helps to know a little of its history, not least because this part of Wales ('Cymru' in Welsh) has been populated since prehistoric times and bears the scars of millennia of occupation. Neanderthals lived here thousands of years ago, possibly up to 200,000 years, living in a high-stress, high-trauma environment, inhabiting caves and hunting wolf, bear and bison. Celtic peoples arrived in Britain about 2,500 years ago and may in time have come to take to a less nomadic existence, settling down and practising transhumance, spending winter months in the valleys but moving to higher pastures during the summer months.

The Romans ventured into Wales and exploited its mineral wealth, but do not appear to have built forts in the region or made significant inroads into the hinterland. As elsewhere in Britain, in the decades following their departure in the 5th century, this part of Wales became a disputed and uneasy arena. In the early 7th century, King Æthelfrith of Northumbria defeated the Welsh in a battle at Chester and massacred the monks assembled to aid the Welsh fighters by prayer. Those that did escape slaughter found their way to the island of Bardsey off the Lleyn Peninsula.

A century later, the Anglo-Saxon King Offa of Mercia (757-796) built a huge earthwork, broadly following the border with Wales from north (Prestatyn) to the south (near Chepstow) as a defence against the Welsh. The seemingly omnipresent Vikings made few inroads into Wales, concentrating on plundering the coastal settlements. They were eventually defeated by the so-called 'King of Wales', Rhodri Mawr, according to the Chronicle of the Princes, 'in hard battle' on Anglesey (Ynys Môn).

Shortly after Wales was first united, in the 10th century, the English started to make encroachments. Gruffudd ap Llywelyn, drove them out and had a stronghold at Rhuddlan. But battles between the Welsh and the Normans continued for many years. Edward I built new castles and the English colonised his fortified towns. Unrest continued until in 1400, Owain Glyndŵr led his rebellion

Heading for Castell Dinas Bran

against English rule, burning several towns in the Vale of Clwyd. It was a war that would last more than ten years, and peace did not finally come to the region until Henry Tudor (Henry VII) seized the crown in 1485 at the culmination of the Wars of the Roses at the Battle of Bosworth Field. But it was not until the English Parliament passed a series of laws between 1536 and 1543, known as the Acts of Union, that Wales and England were politically united.

The Dee Valley
The River Dee encompasses a glorious area of outstanding landscapes that are visited in this guide. Here there are lush green dales, riverside walks, cathedrals and medieval castles. For centuries it was the traditional boundary of the Kingdom of Gwynedd, quite possibly since the 5th century. From its source on the slopes of Dduallt above Llanuwchlyn, south-west of Bala, the river gathers the waters from the Berwyn Hills, before flowing east through the Vale of Llangollen to Wrexham and reaching the English border at Shocklach from where it winds a serpentine course northwards to Chester. Between its source and Bala Lake the river is known by its Welsh name, Afon Dyfrdwy.

The tidal Dee estuary (Aber Dyfrdwy) is a large estuary where the River Dee flows into Liverpool Bay. The estuary starts near Shotton after a five-mile (8

Basingwerk Abbey

km) 'canalised' section, the river swelling to be several miles wide and forming the boundary between the Wirral Peninsula in north-west England and Flintshire in north-east Wales.

Clwydian Hills
Hosting Offa's Dyke, roughly along the border between England and Wales, the Clwydian Hills, a dramatic upland frontier, delineated the ancient boundary between Anglian Mercia and the Welsh kingdom of Powys. Extending from Llandegla in the south to Prestatyn in the north, with the highest point being the popular Moel Famau, the range forms part of the Clwydian Range and Dee Valley Area of Outstanding Natural Beauty, so designated in 1985.

The AONB extends over 150 square miles (390km^2), and all the hills embraced within it offer extensive views across northern Wales, into Snowdonia and east across the Cheshire Plain to the Peak District. There is abundant evidence of prehistoric occupation of the hills in the form of Iron Age hillforts including, for example, Moel Hiraddug, Moel-y-gaer, Penycloddiau and Moel Arthur. That last name also serves to link the hills with legends associated with King Arthur. There is a high probability that the summits of the Clwydian Hills served as a trade route during the Bronze Age.

To the south, the undulating Llandegla moors give way to the expansive Ruabon Mountain and the spectacular limestone cliffs of the

Eglwyseg escarpment. In 2011, the area covered by the AONB was extended southwards to cover the stretch of the Dee valley from Corwen east through the Vale of Llangollen to Newbridge.

North East Wales
To the east of the Clwydian Hills, the rolling countryside of Denbighshire and Flintshire leads to the meandering Dee and the English border. In the Middle Ages, Chester, the major town on the River Dee, was the base from which several English invasions of Wales were launched. The narrow coastal strip along the Dee was by far the easiest route of conquest. So, a series of castles were built along it, including the first two – Flint and Rhuddlan – built by Edward I during his conquest of Wales in the late 13th century. Another outstanding castle was built at Chirk, continually modernised and occupied since it was built, with the intention of keeping the Welsh under English rule.

Apart from medieval castles, other monuments of historic importance range from prehistoric hillforts to the atmospheric ruins of Valle Crucis Abbey. The industrial revolution, too, has left its mark, and no-one can fail to be impressed by Thomas Telford's soaring aqueducts at Pontcysyllte and Chirk.

Walking in the area
Read carefully the general descriptions of each of the walks, their distances and approximate times and decide which best

The remains of Valle Crucis Abbey

suits your purpose, your level of ability and experience and fitness, but keep an eye, too, on the weather forecast. With its magnificent and varied scenery and wealth of historic attractions, it is hardly surprising that this part of Wales has a dedicated popularity; arguably less well-known than other parts of Wales. It is probably true that for every ten visitors to North Wales, only one is heading for the region covered by this guide.

The selection of walks in this guide, which range from 2 to 9 miles, will demonstrate why it deserves to be better known providing, as they do, a balance of easy, moderate and challenging rambles, from the entirely flat walk beside the Afon Clwyd from Rhyl to Rhuddlan, to long and steady ascents of the Arans and the two main Berwyn Hills.

There is an abundance of birdlife here too, including black grouse in Coed Llandegla, passing osprey, and red kite that may have strayed up from central Wales. A pair of binoculars is always a useful addition to your rucksack.

> This book includes a list of waypoints alongside the description of the walk, so that you can enjoy the full benefits of gps should you wish to. For more information about route navigation, improving your map reading ability, walking with a GPS and for an introduction to basic map and compass techniques, read Pathfinder® Guide *Navigation Skills for Walkers* by outdoor writer Terry Marsh (ISBN 978-0-319-09175-3). This title is available in bookshops and online at os.uk/shop

Looking across to the Clwydian Hills from near Rhuddlan

Short walks up to 2½ hours

walk 1

Coed y Gopa

Start
Abergele, off Tan y Gopa road, Conwy

Distance
2 miles (3km)

Height gain
690 feet (210m)

Approximate time
1¼ hours

Route terrain
Woodland trails and paths, some narrow paths with tree roots

Parking
At start (a rough and uneven parking area)

OS maps
Landranger 116 (Denbigh & Colwyn Bay), Explorer 264 (Vale of Clwyd/Dyffryn Clwyd))

GPS waypoints
- SH 933 771
- Ⓐ SH 936 770
- Ⓑ SH 934 771
- Ⓒ SH 935 766
- Ⓓ SH 937 766

The delightful Coed y Gopa – a name that combines the Welsh language for 'wood' and 'summit' – cloaks a limestone knoll in the Vale of Clwyd overlooking the coastal town of Abergele. The woodland, a Site of Special Scientific Interest, is in the care of the Woodland Trust and is a habitat for abundant flora and fauna, coastal views, a glimpse of Gwrych Castle and other historical features. The height gain, such as it is, comes in easy gradients though the main trail is often stony underfoot, and one section within the woodland passes above a steep drop where the path is festooned with tree roots. The walk, in spite of its brevity, is a delightful introduction to the region covered in this guide.

From the parking area, turn through a stile and gate onto a rising stony track that soon yields seaward views over the town of Abergele. The track curves round, with several more opportunities to take in the view. Rising steadily, the track comes to a wooden seat on the left, at an acute right bend Ⓐ. Take this, still rising gently and walking up to a large mound Ⓑ on the right, from the top of which there are fine views that also include Gwrych Castle, which featured in the television series *I'm A Celebrity ... Get Me Out Of Here!*

Coed y Gopa

Already it will be obvious that the route leads through lush woodland, much of it ancient, although large areas were replanted in the 1950s with beech, European larch and pine while natural regeneration has brought about abundant self-sown broadleaved species. Where sunlight filters through the branches a rich understorey has developed, featuring rowan, yew and hazel while several plants find the conditions to their liking: bramble, ferns, bluebells, enchanter's nightshade, honeysuckle, wood sage and dog's mercury.

What makes Coed y Gopa so special is its richness in wildlife and flowers. Birdlife includes goldcrest, goshawk, great spotted woodpecker, nuthatch, redstart and treecreeper, while Natterer's bat and Daubenton's bat inhabit the old mine workings, part of a history of mining from as long ago as the Roman period when Abergele served as a major trading post along the North Wales coast. Lead and copper were mined here and the remains of some of the mines are still visible – though not very evident – today.

Keep following the main trail, passing a branching path on the left and still climbing as it curves around the southern edge of the woodland. On crossing the high point of the track, the route gently descends through young beech woodland. When the way divides, bear left, and when it next divides, a point marked by a low boulder with embedded waymark on the right **C**, turn right on a narrowing path rising to the summit of the hill.

The summit, which is the site of an Iron Age hillfort (Castell Cawr), is undistinguished but located close by a three-way path junction. Go forward on the middle of the three ongoing paths, which shortly starts to descend, the other two paths having circled round to rejoin it. Before long, when the more prominent trail descends very steeply to the right, leave it by taking to a much narrower path on the left **D**, marked by a warning sign about a steep drop.

This path is beset with tree roots and it is important to take care over the placement of feet. After several views out over the town, you reach and ascend a low limestone step for more root-crossed pathway descending steeply in a few places and passing around the top of an obvious limestone

Coed y Gopa

chasm (Hafn Carreg Galch).

Eventually, the path drops to a track junction. Bear right over a wooden footbridge spanning a narrow gorge, and press on until the path finally emerges down wooden steps onto the broad trail used earlier in the walk. Turn right and retrace your outward steps. ●

COED Y GOPA ● 13

walk 2

Valle Crucis Abbey

Start
Horseshoe Falls car park, Dee Valley, just north of Berwyn Railway Station, west of Llangollen, Denbighshire

Distance
2½ miles (4km)

Height gain
460 feet (140m)

Approximate time
1½ hours

Route terrain
Hill paths, farm tracks and canal towpath

Parking
At start, off B5103 (Pay and Display; toilets)

OS maps
Landrangers 117 (Chester & Wrexham/Wrecsam) and 125 (Y Bala & Lake Vyrnwy/Llyn Efyrnwy), Explorer 255 (Llangollen & Berwyn)

GPS waypoints
- SJ 197 433
- Ⓐ SJ 199 434
- Ⓑ SJ 202 443
- Ⓒ SJ 203 441
- Ⓓ SJ 207 436
- Ⓔ SJ 199 433

Today in ruins, Valle Crucis Abbey, founded by Cistercian monks in 1201, used to be the second wealthiest abbey in Wales, after Tintern. The abbey was lived in until its dissolution in 1537. The pond is the only remaining monastic fishpond in Wales. Opposite is Velvet Hill, its Welsh name, Coed Hyrddyn, meaning 'wood of the long man' which some suggest has been related to a tall skeleton unearthed at the site of the nearby Eliseg's Pillar.

Walking through the birch woodlands of Velvet Hill

 Leave the car park either by walking out to the road and turning right for about 100 yards to a signpost on the left, or follow a grassy path through light woodland (signed for Velvet Hill) to emerge onto the road directly opposite the signpost. Take to the path which soon joins a narrow lane. Turn right and descend slightly to a flight of steps on the left, then climb through light birch woodland, lively in spring with birdsong. Finally, leave the woodland at a step-stile Ⓐ and take to a clear path that rises gently across the southern shoulder of Velvet Hill, mantled in bracken and gorse.

Gradually, the path starts to descend and then run parallel with the A542, the abbey now coming into view. Go forward past a low waymark, and continue past the abbey to finally leave the path not far from a telephone box Ⓑ by dropping to a step-stile just at the road's edge. Descend to and cross the road (with care), and turn right towards the signed entrance to Abbey Farm (tea room, farm shop, butcher, toilets).

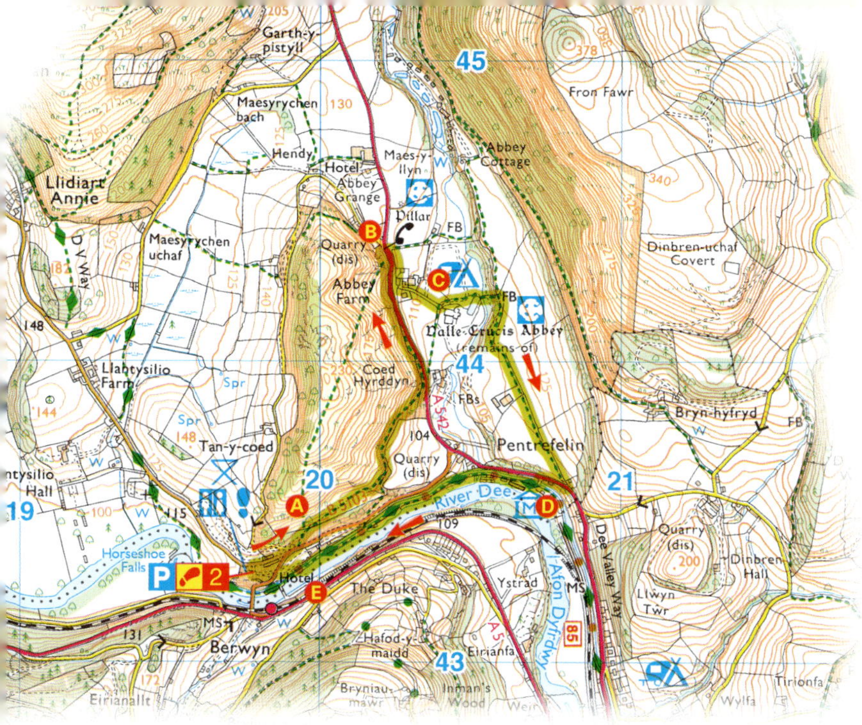

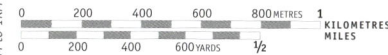

Continue on a lane towards the abbey, now in the care of Cadw (admission charge).

On reaching the abbey **C**, keep left to follow a footpath through a caravan park to locate a footbridge spanning the Eglwyseg river. Over this, take to a steep flight of steps rising to a gate giving onto a broad farm track.

Turn right, descending gently with the track. When it divides keep left and press on to pass a farm, finally dropping easily to intercept the A-road again. Cross the road and turn right, now with the Llangollen Canal in view below. A short way on, leave the road and cross a canal bridge **D**, and over it, turn right to take to the towpath.

Follow the towpath, passing bridge 48AW, and keep forward on a surfaced lane; the canal now cut through bedrock. Just before reaching the **Chainbridge Hotel**, leave the towpath by climbing a large set of iron steps **E**, which span it. Immediately across the canal, bear left on a rising path to the edge of a car park. Turn left and cross a nearby road to gain a path leading back to the car park at the start. ●

Valle Crucis Abbey

Valle Crucis was indisputably Welsh from the moment of its foundation on 28 January 1201 by the lord of Powys Fadog, Madog ap Gruffydd (1191-1236) and the monks of the Cistercian order. Its Latin name (meaning the Valley of the Cross) refers to the nearby 9th-century Pillar of Eliseg (SJ 202 445), erected to the glory of a Welsh chieftain. Such parochial sympathies, no doubt, explain the damage suffered during the wars with the English king, Edward I, and the uprising of Owain Glyndŵr. Even so, it remains one of the best-preserved and atmospheric of Britain's medieval abbeys. From humble beginnings, the abbey later came to be renowned for its profligate hospitality, when ale flowed 'like a river', and food was served in silver dishes.

walk 3

Greenfield Valley Heritage Park

Start
Greenfield, Flintshire

Distance
3 miles (5km)

Height gain
525 feet (160m)

Approximate time
1¾ hours

Route terrain
Woodland paths and tracks, some road walking, old railway trackbed (surfaced)

Parking
At start (adjoining A548)

OS maps
Landranger 116 (Denbigh & Colwyn Bay), Explorer 265 (Clwydian Range/Bryniau Clwyd)

GPS waypoints
- SJ 196 775
- Ⓐ SJ 192 772
- Ⓑ SJ 191 769
- Ⓒ SJ 185 763
- Ⓓ SJ 186 760

Popular with locals but less well known by visiting walkers, the Greenfield Valley is a 70-acre (28-hectare) heritage park full of interest, and with a history extending back to the days when monks began farming the area and pilgrims came to visit the holy well of St Winefride. This was also a busy arena during the Industrial Revolution when cotton and copper mills drew their power from the valley stream. Today this is an appealing, peaceful and wooded area, dotted with reservoirs and industrial remains, the walk concluding along the surfaced trackbed of the Holywell railway.

Leave the car park at its southernmost corner to gain a surfaced lane and almost immediately encounter the enclosed ruins of Basingwerk Abbey (open daily 1000-1600, free admission). Turn right through a metal gate to enter and explore the abbey grounds, and later strike across towards a visitor centre (toilets).

> **Basingwerk Abbey**
>
> Basingwerk Abbey, a daughter house of Combermere Abbey in Cheshire, is but one of a network of Cistercian settlements in Wales. It was founded in 1132 by Ranulf de Gernon, the fourth Earl of Chester, who brought the Benedictines from the Savigny monastery in Normandy. The abbey became part of the Cistercian Order in 1147. Like so many religious houses, Basingwerk fell to the Dissolution of the Lesser Monasteries Act, 1535, and its lands granted to secular owners. Today the abbey is the starting point for the North Wales Pilgrims' Way, a long-distance walking route across the northern part of the country to Bardsey, the so-called 'Island of 20,000 saints'. In 1157, Owain Gwynedd encamped at Basingwerk before facing the forces of Henry II at the Battle of Ewloe, staying in the abbey because of its strategic importance in blocking the route that Henry II had to overcome. In the fighting that followed, Owain defeated the English near Ewloe. By the 13th century, the abbey was under the patronage of Llywelyn the Great, Prince of Gwynedd.

Pass the visitor centre; turn left between buildings, the second of which is the Spring Gardens School. Walk on to pass a children's play area and soon reach The Hatch, a quaint 'snack kiosk', before walking out to meet a lane at a U-bend.

Here, keep left and soon reach a viewpoint on the right for the Abbey Wire Mill. Press on, following a surfaced lane to

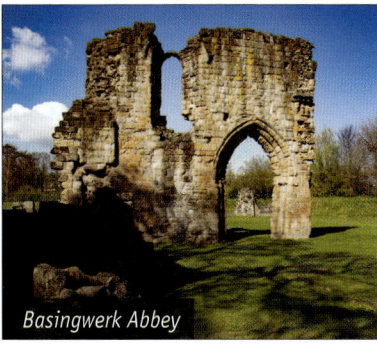

Basingwerk Abbey

pass the site of Lower Cotton Mill **A**. Soon pass a reservoir. When the lane divides (mid-reservoir), keep right. The path soon divides again; keep right once more along a gravel footpath. When the path forks again, at a wrought-iron structure, keep right to reach the site of Meadow Mill **B**. This was the site of the Greenfield Copper and Brass Company's rolling and hammer mill, built in 1787.

At the mill site (information panel), bear left up steps, leaving them at half-height to gain the metal walkway across the end of a dam. On the other side, bear left to enter and cross a car park, on the far side of which a path leads into light woodland cover for a short while. Pass a clock tower (minus its clock), and immediately when the path divides, keep right to pass the site of Greenfield Mills.

At the next junction, keep right alongside an overgrown pool, and when the path next divides, bear left on a gently descending path, at the end of which you pass through a metal arch, engraved 'MOUNT GILEAD MDCCCXXX' (1830) – reference to the Mount Gilead chapel, located on the

SCALE 1:25 000 or 2½ INCHES to 1 MILE 4CM to 1KM

0 200 400 600 800 METRES 1 KILOMETRES

0 200 400 600 YARDS ½ MILES

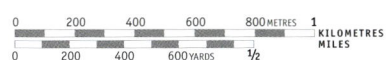

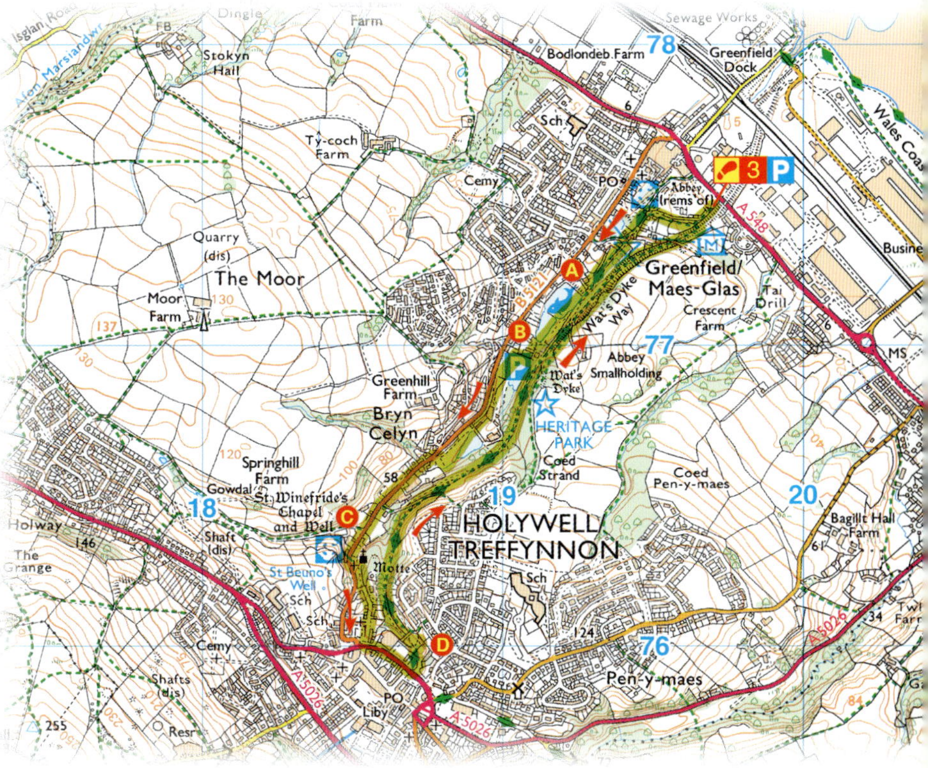

opposite side of the B5121. Here you enter the car park of the **Royal Oak** pub. Turn right up to the B-road, and there turn left to walk along the pavement as far as St Winefride's Chapel and Well C.

St Winefride's Chapel and Well

Reputedly the oldest continually visited pilgrim site in Britain, the holy well at St Winefride's has been a pilgrimage site since 1115, and possibly earlier. The well is believed to spring from the spot where 7th-century Welsh abbot St Beuno brought his niece Winifred back to life, though the tale may in fact have pagan origins. The well has come to be renowned as having healing waters and is known as 'The Lourdes of Wales'. The chapel itself dates from the late 15th century.

Continue up the road to pass a rather Potteresque building and then immediately turn left towards the chapel. On doing so, turn right up a short flight of steps to walk up a pathway along the edge of a living churchyard, part of a network of burial grounds managed for the benefit of people and wildlife. On exiting the graveyard, keep forward uphill, eventually to reach a road junction.

Holywell

This short uphill section is Well Street, the oldest part of Holywell, dating from a time when the town developed around the well. Daniel Defoe visited in 1727 describing it as 'a little town ... which may, indeed, be said to have risen from the confluence of the people hither, for almost all the houses are either publick (sic) houses, or let into lodgings'. Defoe also commented that the story of St Beuon's miracle '...[smelt] too much of legend, to take up any of [his] time'. New town houses were built along Wells Street from the 1760s.

Turn left and walk past a large supermarket, immediately after which, turn left down a road feeding into the car park, but soon leave it, on the right, for an enclosed path D, signed for 'Greenfield Heritage Park'. Shortly, turn down a zigzagging path to pass beneath a double-arched bridge near the site of the former Holywell railway station.

Holywell Railway

The Holywell railway, a mere two miles (3.2km) in length, was opened in 1864, running from the town to a new harbour on the Dee estuary. Conveying only minerals it operated for just a decade before falling into disuse.

Having passed beneath the bridge, now simply follow the surfaced trackbed, ignoring all deviating paths to arrive directly above the site of Basingwerk Abbey. Here the track curves round to meet the route used at the start of the walk, and a brief stroll back to the car park.

Following the old railway trackbed through Greenfield Heritage Park

Northop

Northop is a pleasant village with an ancient pedigree; there is evidence that a church existed here in the 6th century. The present church is not so old, but its churchyard still houses the old grammar school of Northop, which was constructed during the 16th century. The nearby village of Soughton (Sychdyn in Welsh) was listed in the Domesday Book. The walk begins across a golf course near the country-house-cum-hotel of Soughton Hall and then makes an easy circuit of quiet lanes and, for a while, follows the course of Wat's Dyke, an ancient earthwork. The walk is especially delightful in springtime, when the hedgerows are bright with wildflowers and birdsong.

Start	Northop, Flintshire
Distance	3 miles (5km)
Height gain	195 feet (60m)
Approximate time	1¾ hours
Route terrain	Golf course pathways, farm pastures, some road walking
Parking	At start
OS maps	Landranger 117 (Chester & Wrexham/Wrecsam), Explorers 265 (Clwydian Range/Bryniau Clwyd) and 266 (Wirral & Chester)
GPS waypoints	SJ 245 683 Ⓐ SJ 246 679 Ⓑ SJ 239 674 Ⓒ SJ 237 676

Leave the car park at its southern end and cross the road with care to a kissing-gate opposite giving access to the edge of Northop Country Park Golf Club, designed by former Ryder Cup player, John Jacobs. The route forward across the golf course is waymarked – up to a point – a wide grassy path that fades before reaching the green of the fairway on the left (east) side. The right of way crosses the fairway before reaching the green, but if there are players present it may be considered safer to keep forward instead, to pass the tee for the following fairway and go forward to meet a fence, turning left along this. The target either way is a kissing-gate in a field corner Ⓐ.

Cross a surfaced lane at the entrance to Lower Soughton Hall, and through another gate onto an enclosed path. When the broad path bends to the right, leave it and pass through a waymarked kissing-gate on the left, soon crossing a stone bridge; and taking to a pleasant narrow, enclosed path, for some of its length following a stream on the right. When the path divides, bear right beneath a single-arched bridge. The entire path is delightful to walk, passing round the boundary of Soughton Hall Country House Hotel.

> **Soughton Hall** Today a luxury hotel, Soughton Hall, built in 1714, is a Grade II listed building. Notable guests are said to have included Luciano Pavarotti, Michael Jackson and King Juan Carlos I of Spain.

Continue following the path until it finally emerges onto a tree-flanked lane at a bend. Turn right, shortly passing the lodge entrance to Soughton Hall and pressing on to finally reach the A5119. Turn right along the A-road for about 200 yards before branching left onto a minor lane that follows the course of Wat's Dyke and Wat's Dyke Way.

> **Wat's Dyke**
>
> Wat's Dyke (Clawdd Wat) is a 40-mile (64-km) linear earthwork running from Basingwerk Abbey (see Walk 3) on the River Dee estuary, passing east of Oswestry and on to Maesbury in Shropshire, England. Today, the dyke consists of the customary bank and ditch construction, with the ditch on the western side, meaning that the dyke faces Wales and by implication can be seen as protecting the English lands to the east. The dyke is thought to date from 792-852 and in part may be built on a sub-Roman earthwork.

Continue until the lane bends left distinctly **B**, and here cross a low fence stile on the right to access a delightful grassy track flanked in springtime with daffodils, primrose, red campion, celandine, bluebells and selfheal. At the end of the path, cross another stile, and maintain the same direction across the corner of a field to another step-stile. After this, keep forward alongside a fence and when this ends continue in the same direction following an open, more pronounced and elevated section of Wat's Dyke to locate a stile within a group of sycamore and gorse **C**.

Over the stile, go down a path on the left to another stile. Do not cross this stile; do not be drawn into the tempting, enclosed fenced path running off to the right. Instead, keeping the fences to the left, follow the course of the path to a stile in a field corner. As you approach the stile, so Northop church comes into view.

Over the stile keep forward, to the right of a fence and hedge, shortly going through a dip and passing a pond to reach a field gate. Turn through the gate and go forward past a large cottage, and then walk out along the cottage drive to meet a surfaced lane. Turn right, and pass The Green, after which the lane descends to a road junction. Cross the road, entering the road opposite, and walk as far as **The Boot Inn**, and there turn right into Brook Street. Shortly, cross the eponymous brook – an attractive feature – beyond which a main road is encountered. Turn left, cross the A-road at traffic lights, and stroll the short distance to complete the walk.

Following a quiet lane

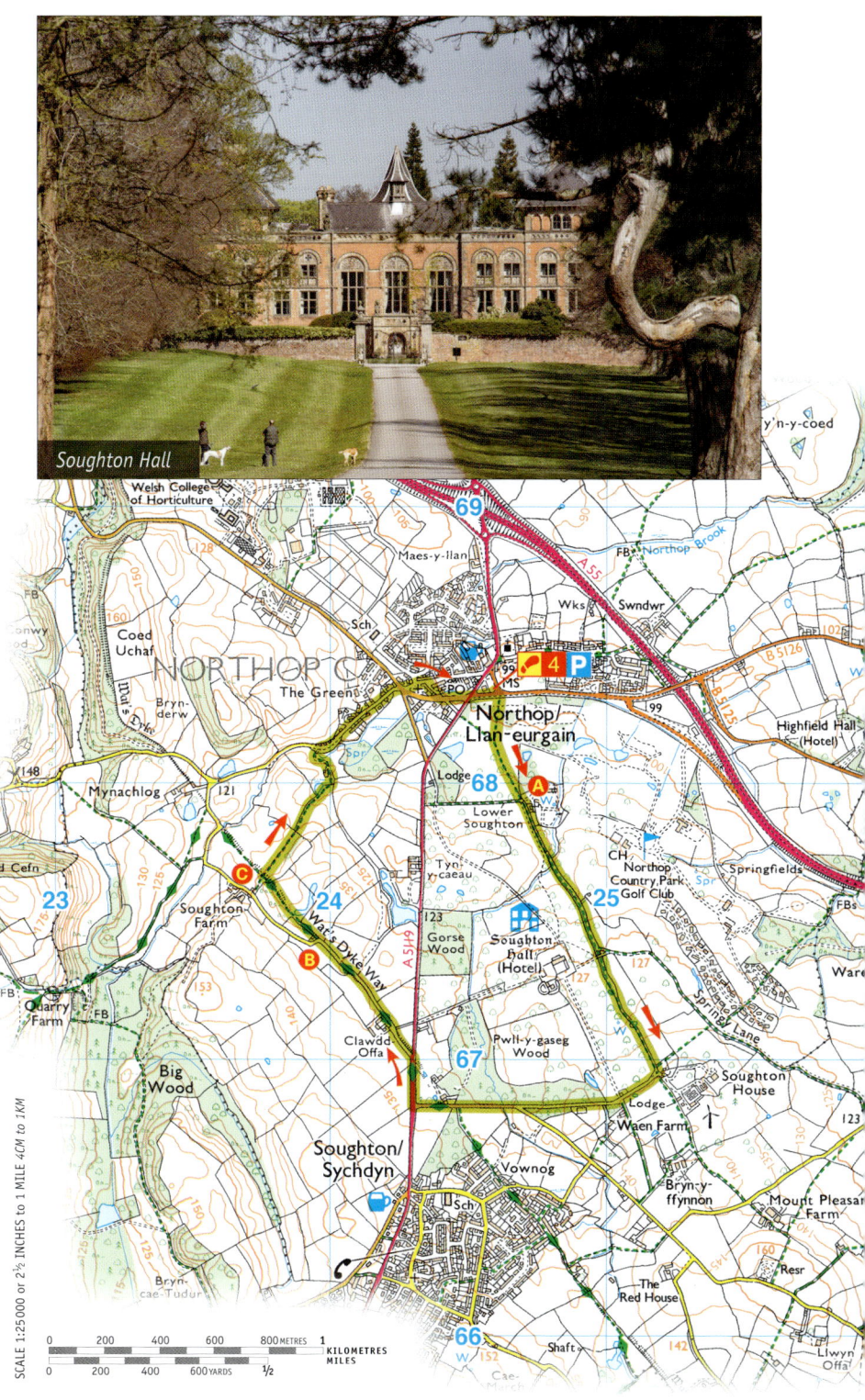

walk 5

St Asaph and Afon Elwy

Start
St Asaph, Denbighshire

Distance
3 miles (5km)

Height gain
215 feet (65m)

Approximate time
1¾ hours

Route terrain
Town centre, minor lanes, farm fields and flood embankment

Parking
Car park at start, Lower Street

OS maps
Landranger 116 (Denbigh & Colwyn Bay), Explorer 264 (Vale of Clwyd/Dyffryn Clwyd)

GPS waypoints
- SJ 036 743
- Ⓐ SJ 034 755
- Ⓑ SJ 032 760
- Ⓒ SJ 032 750

From this ancient cathedral city, the walk runs northwards to access lush farmland and several ancient highways before linking up with the River Elwy for a leisurely return in company with the river.

Leave the car park and walk out to the main road, there turning left and walking uphill to pass the cathedral.

> **St Asaph Cathedral**
>
> The Anglican Cathedral Church of Saints Asaph and Cyndeyrn, commonly called St Asaph Cathedral, dates back 1,400 years, when a community was founded here by the Scottish saint, Kentigern. The current building dates from the reign of Henry Tudor but greatly remodelled in the 19th century; it has twice been destroyed by fire and has a fascinating and violent history, including attacks by rebellious native Welsh people and foreign invaders. Destroyed by the forces of Henry III in 1245 and by the armies of Edward I in 1282, the cathedral was rebuilt between 1284 and 1381 only to be burned by Owain Glyndŵr's Welsh troops in 1402. In 1715 the tower was completely demolished in a fierce storm.

At the crossroads, turn left into Mount Road and follow this as it bends right and left and soon crosses above the A55. Continue past Pen-y-bryn farm and then, as soon as the lane starts to descend steeply, leave it, just past a bench, over a step-stile on the right Ⓐ.

Turn along the left-hand field edge to another stile in a field corner and a few strides later pass through an ancient field boundary. Now move half-right and aim for a low waymark in an ancient boundary. From this cross more pastures on unmarked pathways to gradually home in on the cluster of buildings at Pentre Uchaf farm, approaching this along what appears to be an ancient sunken trackway.

Cross a stile and pass through the farmyard and then turn left along its access to walk out as far as a footbridge on the right crossing the River Elwy Ⓑ. Over the bridge, turn left and shortly up steps to gain the flood embankment.

Now follow this back towards St Asaph. When you can cross the river by a bridge Ⓒ, move to the opposite bank and continue in parallel with the river, this time passing beneath the A55, until a deviating path runs left back to the starting point. ●

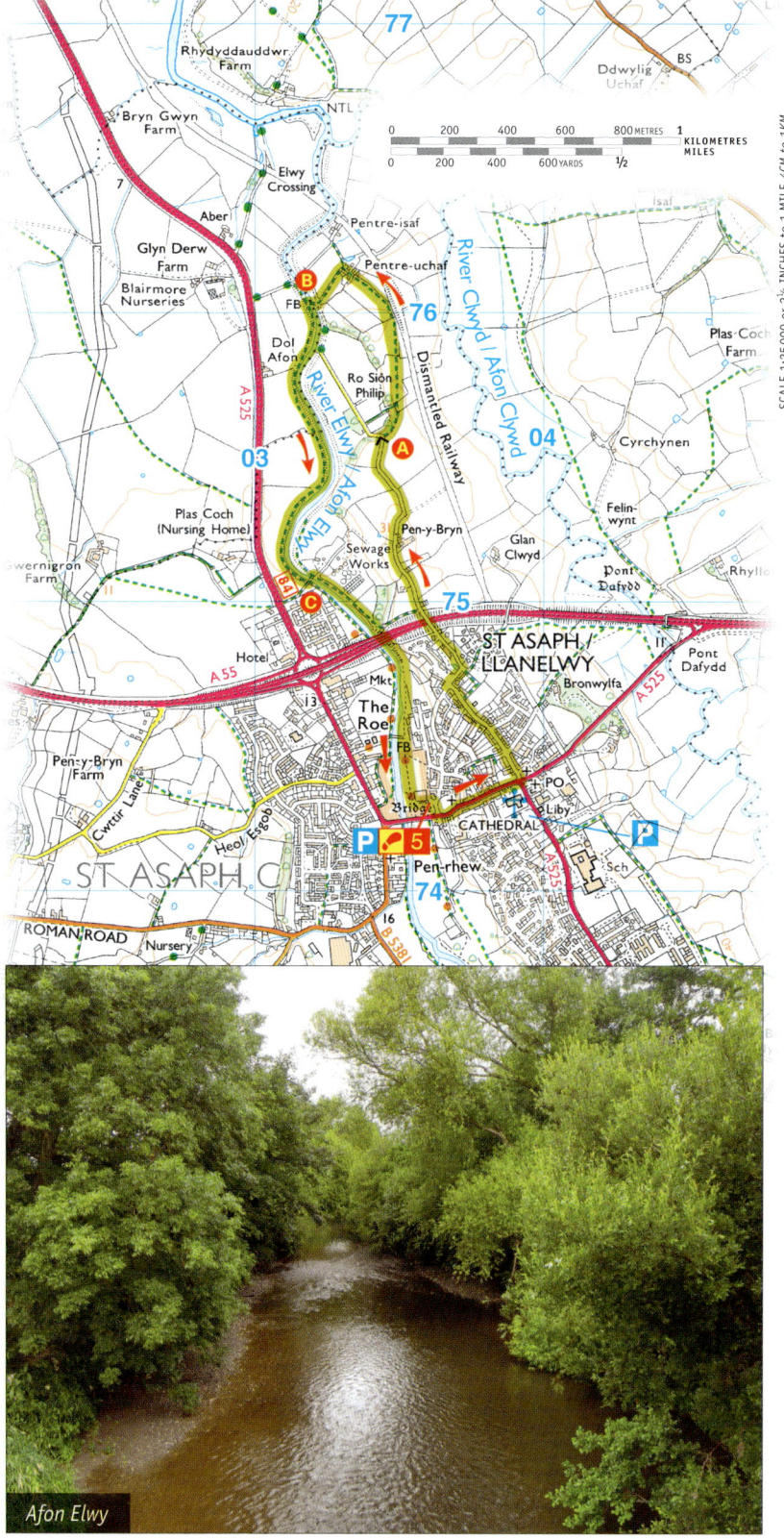

Afon Elwy

ST ASAPH AND AFON ELWY

walk 6

Great Orme

Start
Great Orme Country Park, signposted from centre of Llandudno. Alternatively come on either the Cabin Lift or Tramway from Llandudno, Conwy

Distance
3¼ miles (5.25km)

Height gain
625 feet (190m)

Approximate time
2 hours

Route terrain
Undulating rocky and grassy landscapes; some road walking

Parking
Car park at start

OS maps
Landranger 115 (Snowdon/Yr Wyddfa), Explorer OL17 (Snowdon/Yr Wyddfa)

GPS waypoints
- SH 765 833
- Ⓐ SH 774 830
- Ⓑ SH 770 837
- Ⓒ SH 757 840

The familiar and distinctive headland of the Great Orme rises to 679 feet (207m) above the elegant resort of Llandudno and its summit, from where the walk starts, can be reached by chairlift and tramway from the town centre as well as by car. Most of it is now a country park and on this short circuit there is a succession of outstanding views that take in Llandudno and its curving bay, the Conwy Estuary, mountains of Snowdonia, the Menai Strait and the island of Anglesey. Historic interest is provided by the Great Orme Mines and St Tudno's Church.

As well as the superb views, attractions on the Great Orme range from Bronze Age copper mines and a Dark Age Christian site to the Edwardian tramway, first opened in 1902, and modern chairlift and dry ski-slope.

Head for the Visitor Centre and turn down the road, tramway on your left. Join the grassy path to the right of the road; as the road bends left this path continues down alongside a wall (marked by low marker posts with a white 'walker' on), shortly passing a Great Orme Historical Trail Information Board. At a fingerpost in bracken, keep right to drop to a tarred lane just above the Great Orme Mines. These are old copper mines, first worked in at least 1580BCE and as such the oldest known metal-working site in Britain. Turn right, ignore the left fork to the mine and shortly bend left along the roughening track that passes above the Visitor Centre. Remain on this track through a metal gate and past houses. Go ahead on the tarred lane and bear left to reach a junction Ⓐ at St Beunos Road and the main road carrying the steep tram tracks.

Turn left uphill, go through the gate beside a cattle-grid and then turn right, cross the tramway and walk along the rough lane signed as a footpath for St Tudno's Church. At the fork in 50 paces, keep right on the gravel lane, walking through to a turning area at Pink Farm. Look right here for a kissing-gate and multiple fingerposts, go through this and turn left. Pass through a metal gate behind the farm and cottage and go ahead along a fenced track. Passing a field gate, this narrows to a path; go through two kissing-gates and keep ahead to reach a lane and St Tudno's Church Ⓑ.

Turn uphill and wind with the road above the sloping graveyards. About 50 yards beyond the upper boundary wall,

St Tudno's Church

fork right through some roadside boulders onto a wide grassy path through bracken. This cuts through to a sheep-cropped grass common; bear right up across this to find a gravel lane and turn right, shortly picking up a stone estate wall on your left. This is your constant companion for the remainder of the walk. There are excellent views across the Irish Sea; on very clear days the Isle of Man and the Lake District's mountains can be seen.

At a wall corner **C** turn left, continue beside it and follow it as it curves left again. Now come possibly the finest views of the walk, looking across the Conwy Estuary to Conwy town and castle, with the panorama of the Snowdonia mountains visible on the horizon to the south.

Keep beside the wall where it turns left again and head uphill to return to the start.

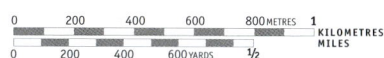

SCALE 1:25000 or 2½ INCHES to 1 MILE 4CM to 1KM

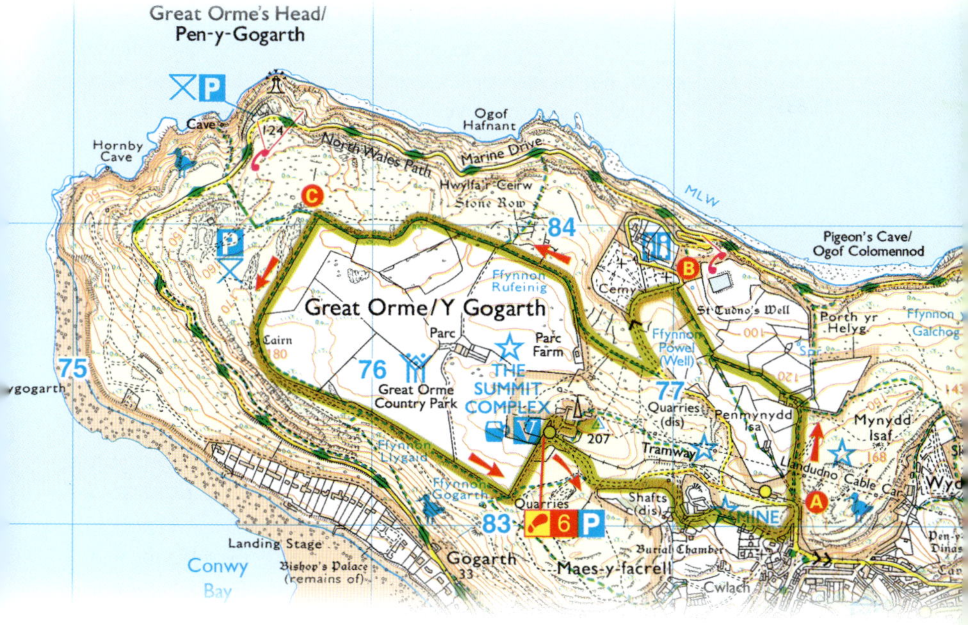

GREAT ORME • 25

walk 7

Castell Dinas Bran

Start
Llangollen, Denbighshire

Distance
3 miles (5km)

Height gain
855 feet (260m)

Approximate time
2 hours

Route terrain
Town pavement, hill paths, minor roads

Parking
Mill Street car park at start (Pay and display)

OS maps
Landranger 117 (Chester & Wrexham/Wrecsam), Explorer 255 (Llangollen & Berwyn)

GPS waypoints
- SJ 217 421
- Ⓐ SJ 216 428
- Ⓑ SJ 227 432

The ascent of Castel Dinas Bran from Llangollen has the distinction that, apart from very short stretches, every step is uphill; thankfully, not remorsefully so and in the upper reaches what appears on first sight as a daunting proposition is eased by a series of zigzags. The hill on which the ancient castle sits is not especially high, but it commands an outstanding view north to the stunning escarpment of Creigiau Eglwyseg and north-west to Llantysilio Mountain (Walk 24).

Castell Dinas Bran

From the bottom of the car park, take the Riverside Path towards the town centre and shortly bear right up steps to the A539. Head towards the **Bridge End Hotel** and just before it turn right to follow a road, swinging left to climb up to the Llangollen Canal (Walk 11). Cross the canal bridge and go forward up steps on a signed path for Castell Dinas Bran, a surfaced way between fences flanked by hedge cranesbill and feverfew among several other colourful plants that bloom in spring and summer.

The path leads up to a surfaced lane. Cross this and continue ascending along a field edge to a kissing-gate giving onto an access track. This in turn leads up past Fourways Cottage Ⓐ, continuing as a gravel track up to a 'Crow' gate, giving onto the slopes of Dinas Bran: the name has variously been translated as 'Crow's Castle' or 'Crow's Fortress'.

Through the gate, bear right and soon reach a level plateau – make the most of this by pausing to take in the inspiring and colourful views. Directly ahead, Dinas Bran looms, but the onward route takes to a clear path that zigzags up the steep profile to enter the surprise world of ruins that is Castell Dinas Bran.

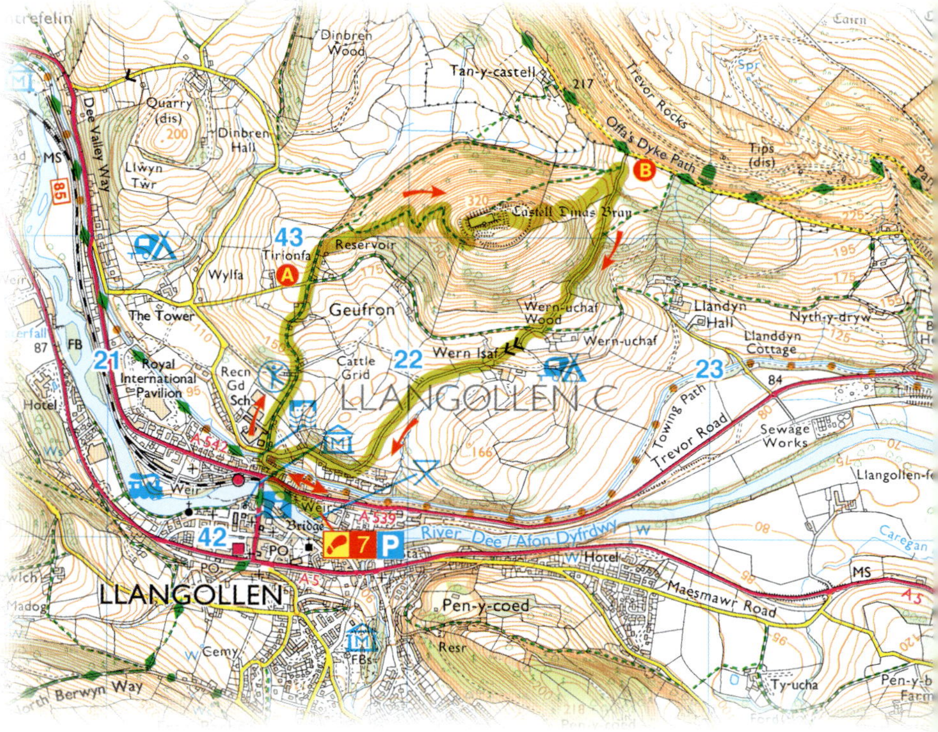

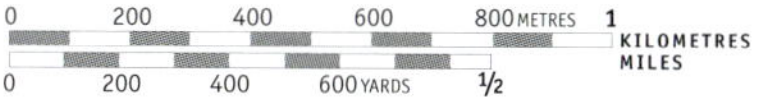

> ### Castell Dinas Bran
>
> The castle is thought to have been built originally in the 1260s by a prince of Powys Fadog, Gruffydd Maelor, but it almost certainly stands on the site of a wooden castle and an even earlier Iron Age hillfort dating from more than 2,500 years ago, built by a Celtic tribe known as the Ordovices. In 1277, Edward I of England launched his Conquest of North Wales and it was about this time that the castle was destroyed and abandoned by the occupying allies of Llywelyn Prince of Wales.

Having explored the castle leave it at the eastern end and go down grassy slopes that feed into a gravel and stepped path, passing through gates before finally crossing a low gorsey rise and arriving at a minor lane ⓑ. Turn right to follow the lane all the way back to Llangollen. *There is scope for those wanting a longer walk to turn briefly left to a T-junction and then right, following a lane in the direction of Trevor Uchaf where, on crossing the A539, it becomes possible to join the canal towpath and follow this back to town.*

The original descending lane is narrow and occasionally steep, but it is blessed with a wide variety of wildflowers including musk mallow, hedgerow cranesbill, purple toadflax, honeysuckle, ladies bedstraw and many more.

Follow the lane to its end at the canal bridge crossed at the start of the walk, and retrace outward steps to the car park.

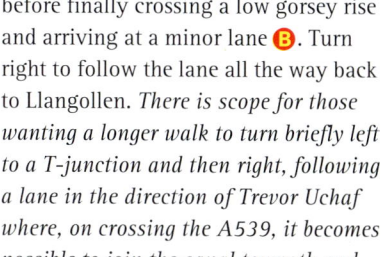

SCALE 1:25000 or 2½ INCHES to 1 MILE 4CM to 1KM

walk 8

Llannefydd and Mynydd y Gaer

Start
Llannefydd, Conwy

Distance
3½ miles (5.6km)

Height gain
690 feet (210m)

Approximate time
2 hours

Route terrain
Country lanes, farm and field tracks

Parking
At start (toilets)

OS maps
Landranger 116 (Denbigh & Colwyn Bay), Explorer 264 (Vale of Clwyd/Dyffryn Clwyd)

GPS waypoints
- SH 981 706
- **A** SH 977 709
- **B** SH 973 713
- **C** SH 972 721
- **D** SH 975 713

The pleasing village of Llannefydd, part of Conwy District, lies in the middle of an undulating landscape of low hills and valleys to the south of Bodelwyddan close to the Denbighshire border between the Afon Aled and River Elwy. The village, which has a pleasant pub, the Hawk and Buckle, is remarkable in having no fewer than 38 listed buildings within only a short distance, including a sundial and base at the Church of St Nefydd and St Mary. The walk ambles around the countryside to the north-west of the village, and climbs steadily to a hillfort of late-Prehistoric or Iron Age origin.

Leave the village car park by taking to a signed footpath to the left of the toilets. This proves to be a broad, hedged track that leads up to Pen Bryn Llan, on the way offering pleasing views northwards to the high point of the walk, Mynydd y Gaer. At Pen Bryn Llan, cross a step-stile on the right, and walk downfield to a metal field gate and stile. Keep forward down what appears to be an old sunken lane hedged with hawthorn on the right. Then keep forward towards a large tree and a surfaced lane.

Turn right and walk up to a junction **A**, there turning left and walking as far as an obvious branching lane on the right, at a bend. Bear right and shortly right again to walk up in the direction of the group of buildings at Sychnant. Upon reaching a junction **B**, with two lanes branching off to the right, turn left. Ignore the broad track that runs round to Sychnant, and instead, immediately take to a descending footpath on the left. This leads down to a bridlegate, giving on to a continuing track, a white road, that now circles round the base of Mynydd y Gaer, with pleasant views westwards across the Elwy valley.

The path eventually comes out to join a surfaced lane. Walk forward along this for about 200 yards, to a footpath signpost on the right. [The same point can be reached from where the route joins the lane, by a higher footpath above and parallel with the lane.] From the signpost, turn onto a broad ascending track rising across the northern slopes of Mynydd y Gaer and follow this until it turns south at a bend **C**, an excellent spot for a breather, with good views north and west.

Now head south and uphill on the continuing track to pass Ty-newydd, shortly after which the main track swings left over a cattle-grid to pass round the edge of Access Land to another cattle-grid giving onto a rough surfaced lane. Turn right on this.

From the first cattle-grid, a green path, a variant possibility, rises onto Mynydd y Gaer, which provides a focus of interest.

> **Mynydd y Gaer** The hillfort of Mynydd y Gaer is not large, roughly hexagonal with a diameter of 200 yards and bounded by the remains of ramparts. These hillforts are characteristic of the Iron Age and the late-Prehistoric period, and the more prominent among them may have been used during Roman times.

Anyone visiting the top of Mynydd y Gaer will have no difficulty finding a way eastwards through the ramparts and down to intercept the original route of the walk. From here, the lane soon descends steeply. Ignore branching footpaths and walk down until the lane divides. Now bear left, descending on a white road and passing a cottage before reaching a lane at a Y-junction. Bear right here, and walk down to a corner near Ochor-y-gaer. Here go right, along the lane and walking as far as a signpost on the left **D**. Here, turn acutely left onto an uneven and irregular path through rough shrubbery and alongside a fence.

The path soon reaches a step-stile, and over this go forward into a pasture and alongside a hedge and fence towards a field gate ahead. Just before reaching the gate, cross another step-stile on the right. Walk down the right-hand edge of a sloping pasture flanked by substantial growths of gorse. At the bottom edge of the field, divert left to a field gate, and through this go forward with a hedgerow on the right. When the hedgerow changes direction, turn right through another field gate and head upfield to a gate giving onto the lane into Llannefydd at the junction **A** passed on the outward route. Turn left and walk up into the village to complete the walk. ●

walk 9

Caergwrle and Hope

Start
Caergwrle, Flintshire

Distance
3¾ miles (6km)

Height gain
375 feet (115m)

Approximate time
2 hours

Route terrain
Woodland; some road walking

Parking
Car park at start

OS maps
Landranger 117 (Chester & Wrexham/Wrecsam), Explorer 256 (Wrexham/Wrecsam & Llangollen)

GPS waypoints
- SJ 305 574
- Ⓐ SJ 311 576
- Ⓑ SJ 310 583
- Ⓒ SJ 321 587
- Ⓓ SJ 324 585
- Ⓔ SJ 318 576

Towards the end of this pleasant and easy walk in the Alyn valley, there are fine views of the wooded slopes of Hope Mountain. On such a modest walk there should be enough energy at the end to take you up to the ruins of Caergwrle Castle; it's a grand viewpoint.

Begin by turning left out of the car park along High Street and take the first turning on the right, passing to the right of a church. Follow a narrow lane to a road, cross over and continue along a tarmac track which descends to cross a 17th-century packhorse bridge over the River Alyn. Head uphill between houses and cottages, cross a railway line and descend to a road.

Walk ahead up the concrete drive opposite. Near the top, look on your right for steps up to a kissing-gate, go through this and turn left. Walk outside the property boundary to another kissing-gate ahead. Go through this and turn left along a fenced path Ⓐ. Remain on this path which shortly skirts a line of trees. This is the line of Wat's Dyke. Like the better-known and more extensive Offa's Dyke, this was constructed in the 8th or 9th century as a boundary between the Kingdom of Mercia and the Welsh.

Through a kissing-gate and remain with the fenced path, rising beside a driveway to a road. Turn left, take the first turning on the left and follow a lane up to Hope church. In front of the medieval church turn right along a track Ⓑ to the road, cross over and take the tarmac track opposite. Just after passing a farm, turn left, at a public footpath sign, descend to a stile, climb it and bear right to head diagonally uphill across a field. Descend to climb another stile, and turn right along the right-hand edge of two fields, to another stile. After the next stile, keep along the left edge of the field, turn right in the corner and look for another stile on your left. Cross this and go ahead to a further stile giving onto a grassy track. Keep ahead through a gate, past a cottage to a lane Ⓒ.

Turn right along this and after 400 yards – just after passing a large brick house (Shordley Hall) on the left – turn right over a stile Ⓓ and walk across a field to a metal gate. Go through, continue across the next field, climb a stile and keep ahead to join and keep alongside the left field edge. Go through a gate near the field corner, head diagonally across the next field and descend to go through a gate. Walk the track past ruins and through another gate. As the track turns left, look carefully on

your right for a curious stile across sheathed barbed wire hidden in overgrown bushes. Walk along the right edge of the pasture to a point 30 paces beyond the second pylon; here fork half-left up the bank, pass through the line of old hedge and continue half-right to an unusual three-way stile in the field corner. Bear right along the lane to reach a T-junction **E**. Cross the main road and climb the stile opposite. Walk along the right-hand edge of a field, pass through a hedge gap and keep ahead to the edge of the wooded hill of Caer Estyn, the site of an Iron Age hillfort.

Turn right through two kissing-gates in quick succession and keep along the left edge of a field below the wooded hill. Through another kissing-gate, cross the quarry road and take a kissing-gate into a fenced path that continues to skirt the foot of Caer Estyn. This gradually descends the field edge, with good views ahead across Caergwrle and the Alyn valley to Hope Mountain, right to Hope church and the distant industrial complexes of Deeside.

The path drops to reach the stile near to the point **A** used earlier in the walk. Through the kissing-gate and descend alongside the boundary fence ahead to find the steps down to a concrete drive. Walk down to the road and turn left. Go across the river bridge beside **The Bridge** pub and cross carefully to the right. Pass beneath the railway bridge and turn right along Castle Street. Stay on this to the T-junction with High Street. Here turn right to return to the car park.

A short diversion to the left, however, brings you to a path on the left beside the war memorial, which rises steeply to Caergwrle Castle, a superb viewpoint. The meagre remains are of a late 12th-century castle originally built by Dafydd ap Gruffyd, the brother of Llewellyn ap Gruffyd who was the last independent Prince of Wales. It was later rebuilt by Edward I after his successful Welsh campaigns but abandoned shortly afterwards.

Descend from the castle and walk along High Street back to the start. ●

walk 10

Denbigh and the Ystrad valley

Start
Denbigh, Denbighshire

Distance
5 miles (8km)

Height gain
575 feet (175m)

Approximate time
2½ hours

Route terrain
Urban streets; farmland; riverside paths

Parking
Car parks in Denbigh

OS maps
Landranger 116 (Denbigh and Colwyn Bay), Explorer 264 (Vale of Clwyd/Dyffryn Clwyd)

GPS waypoints
- SJ 050 661
- Ⓐ SJ 050 656
- Ⓑ SJ 057 649
- Ⓒ SJ 054 649
- Ⓓ SJ 044 652
- Ⓔ SJ 032 650
- Ⓕ SJ 049 657

Although a short walk, this route abounds with interest and provides a succession of outstanding views across the Vale of Clwyd. From Denbigh you descend into the valley of the little River Ystrad and follow its course across meadows and through woodland, to the ruins of a small cottage associated with Dr Johnson. Near the end comes a dramatic view of Denbigh Castle, perched on its hill above the town and Vale with the long line of the Clwydian Range on the horizon.

The walled town of Denbigh is dominated by the ruins of its late-13th-century castle. It was built by the powerful Henry de Lacy, Earl of Lincoln, who was entrusted by Edward I with the task of keeping the local area firmly under English control. Apart from its extent, the most impressive feature of the castle is the elaborate three-towered gateway. Most of the town walls, contemporary with the castle, survive, though the modern town has moved down the hill outside them. Within the walls are the remains of two churches. The first is the shell of an Elizabethan cathedral, 'Leicester's Church', intended by Robert Dudley, Earl of Leicester and Lord of Denbigh, to replace the cathedral at St Asaph but never completed. The second is a surviving tower from the medieval town chapel of St Hilary.

The walk begins in the town centre, facing the Library and Museum Gallery. Pass to the right of it, turn right steeply up Bull Lane, go round a right bend and continue up St Hilary's Terrace, passing Leicester's Church. Turn right, then left, passing the tower of St Hilary's Church, and then right again in front of the castle. At a T-junction, turn left below the castle walls, head down to another T-junction Ⓐ and turn left.

At a public footpath sign turn left along an enclosed track, which later narrows to a hedge-lined path. The path descends, but before reaching the bottom, turn right at a footpath sign and walk along the fenced path to use a kissing-gate. From here head half-left, gently downhill across the sloping pasture to the bottom corner and a stile and kissing-gate. Use the stile, put the hedge on your left and walk to and through another kissing-gate; keep the hedge left to reach several gateways at a corner. Go straight on, putting a hedge on your right, and walk on to a stile. Climb this and hug the top of the field to another stile in a corner Ⓑ.

Climb this stile and walk along the wooded path, an occasionally very narrow passage. Climb two stiles before eventually reaching a lane. Turn right, uphill and walk to find a fingerposted track **C** on your left beside a copse.

Turn along this and remain on it, eventually passing in front of a remote house. Beyond here the track shrinks to a wide woodland path, shortly passing through a hand-gate. Remain on this peaceful path just above the River Ystrad to reach an old gate blocking the way. Fork left here, climb the nearby stile and walk the left side of the riverside meadow. Climb another stile and keep ahead, joining the green hollow to the right of a distinct mound. Go through a field gate and ahead past the cottage to a corner stile. Climb this and turn right up the lane.

In 200 yards, double back to the left along a grassy, hedged track **D**. This passes behind a range of estate buildings before becoming a wooded path. Continue on this path, crossing two stile/gates before entering a riverside meadow – on your right is the tree-shrouded ruin of Dr Johnson's Cottage, said to be where the renowned traveller and lexicographer stayed during a tour of Wales. At the end of the meadow go through a kissing-gate into woodland, and immediately fork right up a steep path **E** to the top edge of the trees.

SCALE 1:25 000 or 2½ INCHES to 1 MILE 4CM to 1KM

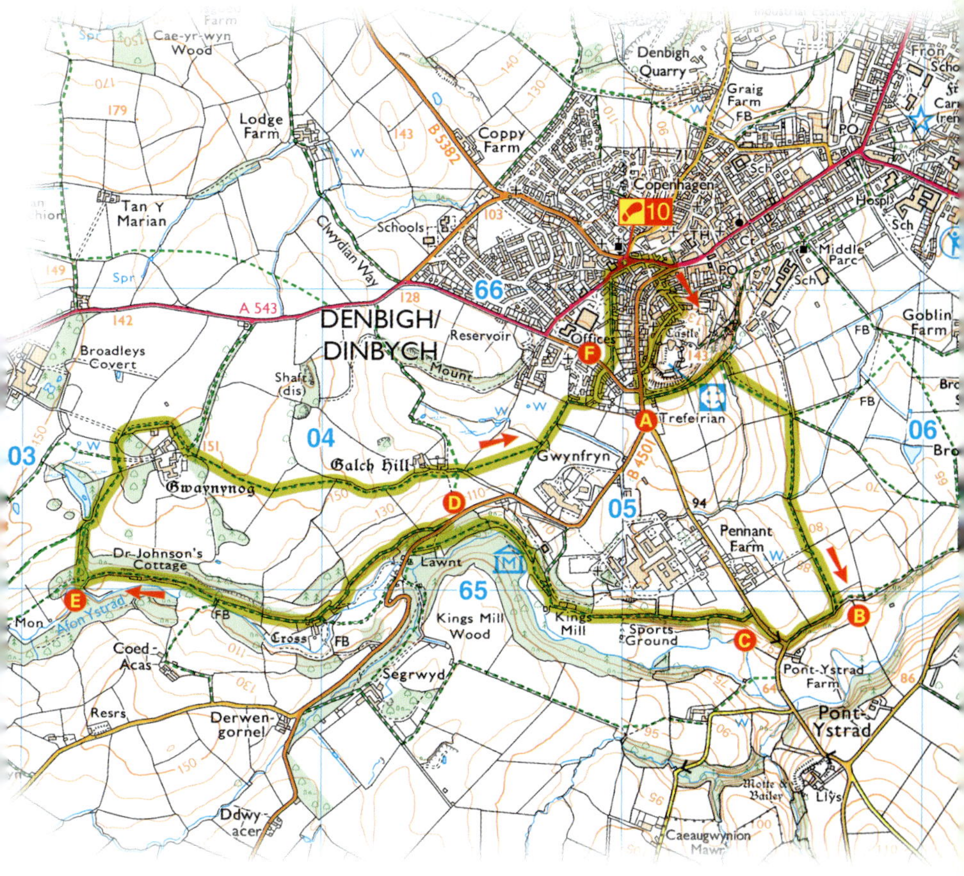

DENBIGH AND THE YSTRAD VALLEY • 33

Denbigh and Denbigh Castle

Climb the stile and turn right up beside the woods; the field funnels into a long entry and another stile. Climb this and bend left (ignore the stile into more woods) on a field track beside a small quarry area that leads to a gateway. Go through this and walk ahead to a stone and slate stile at a wooded corner. Take this and keep right to a farther kissing-gate; once through this, bend right along the edge of the large field outside the estate wall. Use another kissing-gate beside a gate on your right and keep ahead along a dirt road. Cross straight over the driveway to the imposing Gwaynynog Manor (where Beatrix Potter worked on illustrations for her books) and walk on with the field road, grand views of the Clwydian Range drawing the eye ahead.

Pass through another kissing-gate and head a hair's breadth left, aiming for a stile beneath an oak in the far field boundary. From here are excellent views across to Denbigh Castle. Walk along the left side of the field (ignore the stile in 20 paces) to use another stile in 100 yards. Keep to the left of this field to drop to a gate on the left past a cottage. Through this, turn right joining a rough lane. Walk this lane to a finger-posted stone stile on your left. Climb this and walk diagonally right to the far corner and a stone stile beside a gateway (Clwydian Way marker). Use this and trace the right side of the field to take a kissing-gate into an enclosed path behind housing.

This bends left to emerge on an estate road. Turn left to reach a T-junction **F**. Turn right and immediately cross the road to join a tarred path on the left dropping past allotment gardens. Keep ahead on the lane at the bottom to reach a junction. Turn right to return to the centre of Denbigh. ●

A taste of the Llangollen Canal

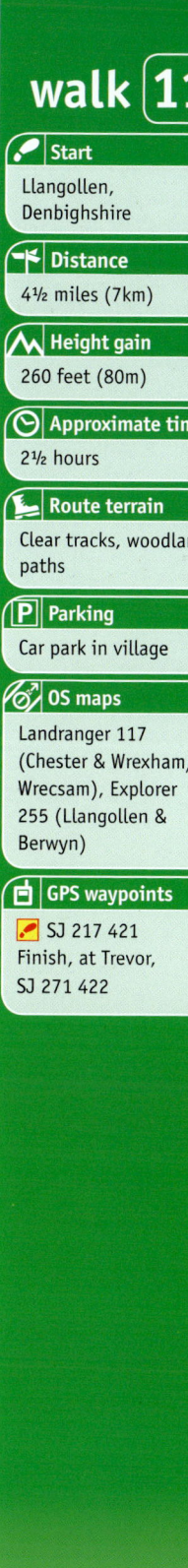

walk 11

Start
Llangollen, Denbighshire

Distance
4½ miles (7km)

Height gain
260 feet (80m)

Approximate time
2½ hours

Route terrain
Clear tracks, woodland paths

Parking
Car park in village

OS maps
Landranger 117 (Chester & Wrexham/Wrecsam), Explorer 255 (Llangollen & Berwyn)

GPS waypoints
SJ 217 421
Finish, at Trevor, SJ 271 422

As might be expected, a walk that is almost entirely alongside a canal is not going to need much in the way of route description; and this is certainly the case with this delightful amble from the centre of Llangollen to the village of Pontcysyllte, renowned for its remarkable aqueduct. The walk is necessarily linear, but if the day is especially pleasant, there is no finer return to Llangollen than to walk back along the canal, from any point in the walk. Traveline Cymru (www.traveline.cymru Tel. 0800 464 0000) details bus services that operate between Trevor, just north of the walk's end at Pontcysyllte, and Llangollen.

Linking Llangollen in Denbighshire with Hurleston in South Cheshire, the Llangollen Canal is a navigable canal, crossing the border between England and Wales. In 2009, 11 miles (17.7km) of the canal, from Gledrid Bridge, near Rhoswiel, to the Horseshoe Falls, which includes Chirk Aqueduct and Pontcysyllte Aqueduct, was declared a World Heritage Site.

The waterway was built when work to complete the Ellesmere Canal was halted in the early 19th century. The Ellesmere Canal was intended to be a commercial waterway linking the Port of Liverpool to the West Midlands. Beset with problems, however, the scheme was never completed. As the waterway never reached its proposed main source of water at Moss Valley, Wrexham, a feeder channel was constructed along the side of the Vale of Llangollen to the River Dee: this work created the Horseshoe Falls at Llantysilio.

Leave the long stay car park in Llangollen, and walk briefly alongside the River Dee towards the town centre, before ascending steps to the road, near the **Bridge End Hotel**. Cross the road with care, and take the first turning on the right, just before the hotel, and on reaching Minffordd, swing to the left, ascending, to reach the canal towpath (seasonal **tea room** nearby). On reaching the canal, turn right beneath Bridge 45W to set off along the towpath.

Initially, the canal is high above the A539, as it ambles easily along with improving vistas off to the left of Castell Dinas Bran (see Walk 7) and the limestone escarpment of Trevor Rocks putting on a fine display. Continue under Bridge 43W and pass

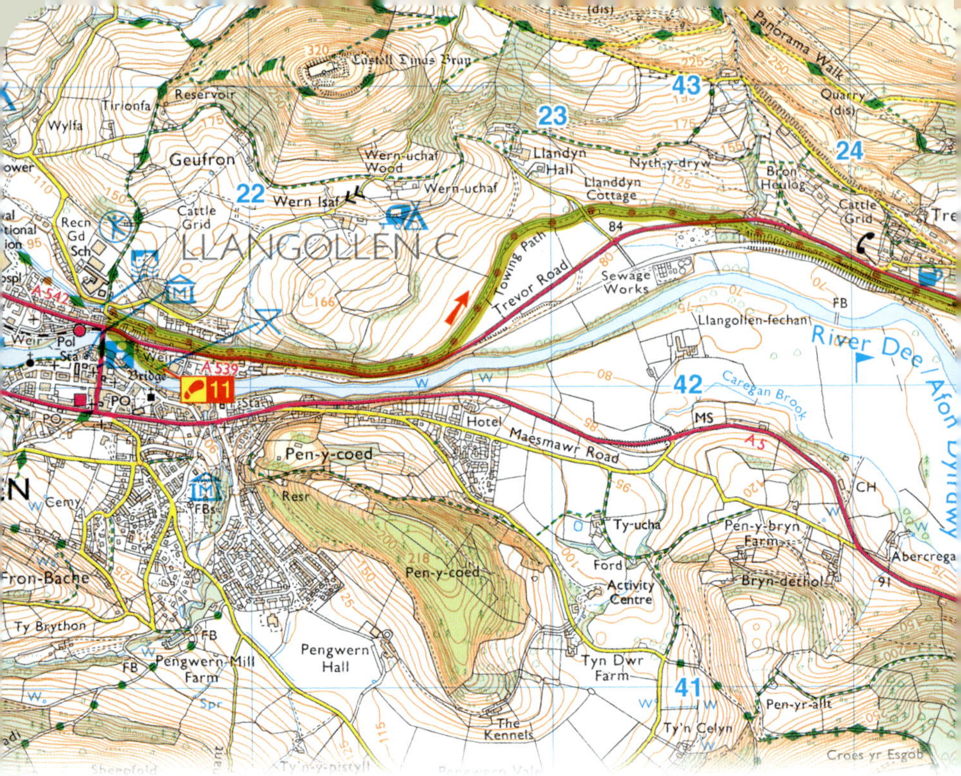

SCALE 1:25000 or 2½ INCHES to 1 MILE 4CM to 1KM

0 200 400 600 800 METRES 1 KILOMETRES
0 200 400 600 YARDS ½ MILES

an isolated cottage. Soon, the canal passes beneath the A-road, and continues its way. Bridge 41W gives access to a hotel called **Sun Trevor**, which serves a range of fine ales and beers and serves food.

Now, with agreeable views ahead and to the south, the canal eases onward, once more switching sides at Bridge 32W. When the towpath emerges onto a road, near Pen-y-bont, cross diagonally left through the basin of Anglo-Welsh Waterway Holidays. Cross the bridge ahead, and turn right to walk to the edge of the famous Pontcysyllte Aqueduct. The aqueduct and canal are early and outstanding examples of innovation inspired by the Industrial Revolution, where they made decisive development in transport capacities possible. It is for this reason that they were accorded World Heritage status. ●

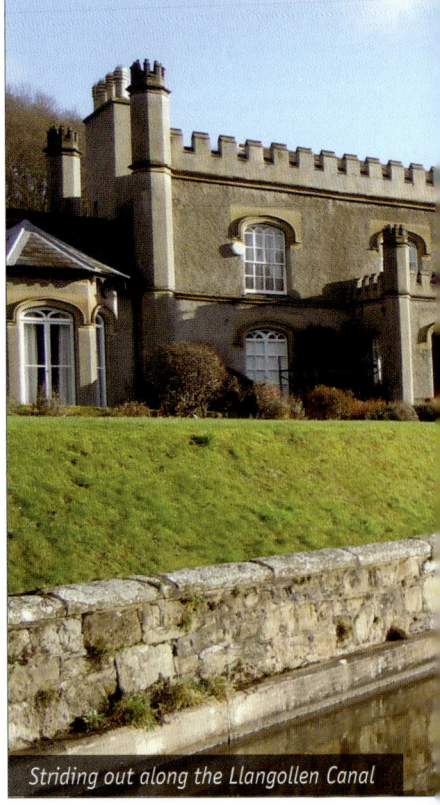

Striding out along the Llangollen Canal

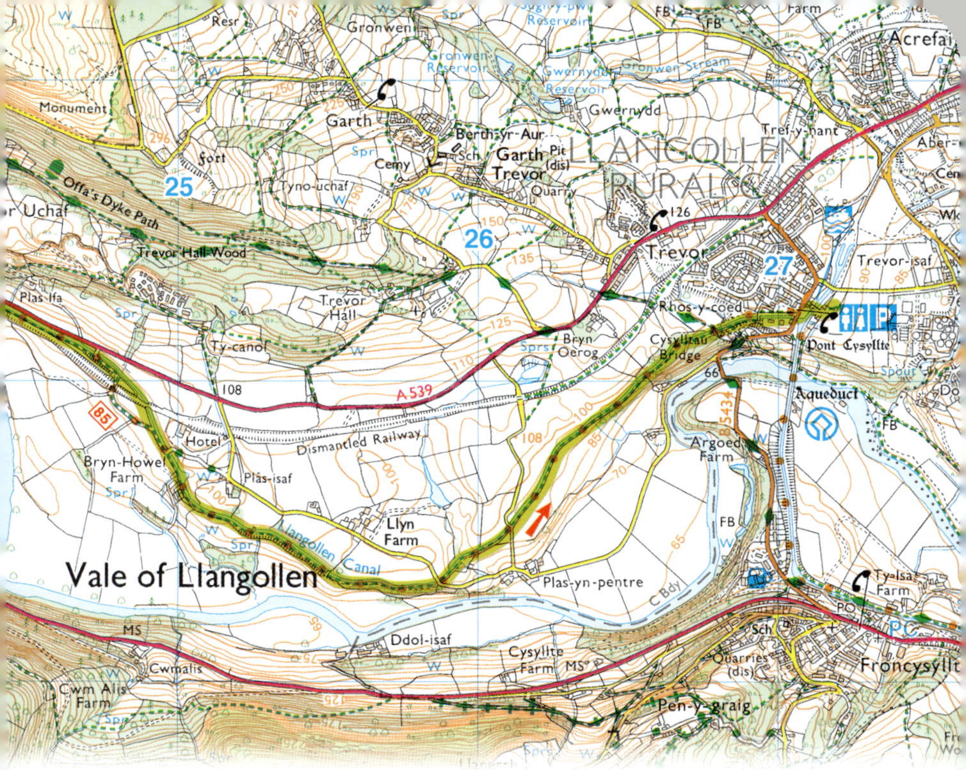
Vale of Llangollen
Llangollen Canal
Trevor
Garth
Froncysyllte
Aqueduct
Pont Cysyllte
A 539
Dismantled Railway
Offa's Dyke Path
Trevor Hall Wood
Trevor Hall
Ty-canol
Hotel
Bryn-Howel Farm
Plâs-isaf
Llyn Farm
Plas-yn-pentre
Ddol-isaf
Cysyllte Farm
Cwmalis
Cwm Alis Farm
Pen-y-graig
Argoed Farm
Rhos-y-coed
Cysylltau Bridge
Bryn Oerog
Trevor-isaf
Tref-y-nant
Gwernydd
Gronwen
Gronwen Reservoir
Gwernydd Reservoir
Berth-yr-Aur
Garth Trevor
Tyno-uchaf
Monument
Fort
Plas Ifa
Acrefair
LLANGOLLEN RURAL
25
26
27
B5434
Ty-Isaf Farm
Quarries (dis)

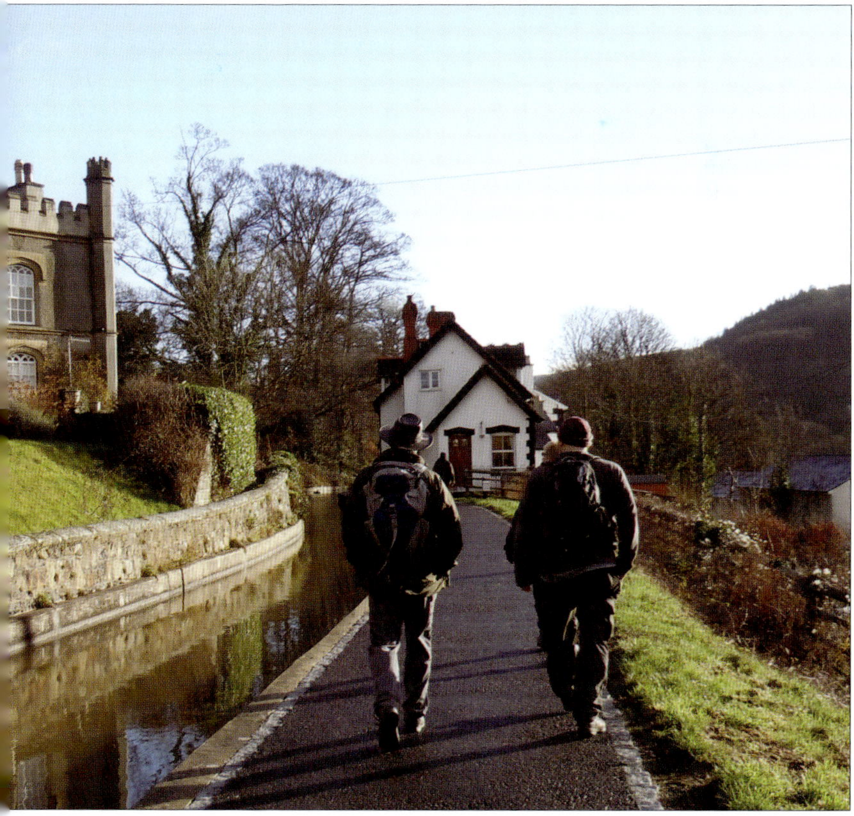

walk 12

Hawarden

Start
Tinkersdale, Hawarden, Flintshire

Distance
4½ miles (7km)

Height gain
460 feet (140m)

Approximate time
2½ hours

Route terrain
Parkland, woodland, farm fields and country tracks

Parking
Tinkersdale car park at start

OS maps
Landranger 117 (Chester & Wrexham/Wrecsam), Explorer 266 (Wirral & Chester)

GPS waypoints
 SJ 315 656
Ⓐ SJ 316 646
Ⓑ SJ 310 637
Ⓒ SJ 310 641
Ⓓ SJ 307 644

Close to the border with England, the clustered village of Hawarden, in the county of Flintshire, has always been of strategic significance as two castles attest, and featured in Henry II's attempt in 1157 to conquer Wales, and later in 1282, when Dafydd ap Gruffudd attacked Hawarden's castle. The 'new' castle, built in the 18th century, was the sometime home of the British Prime Minister, William Ewart Gladstone. This agreeable, easy-moderate walk explores the beauty of Hawarden Park and the farmlands to the west, but walking in the estate (which embraces the entire walk), other than on rights of way, requires a licence to do so, and these are restricted to local residents.

 The walk begins from the Tinkersdale car park via a signed footpath descending to a broad path alongside a fence through Hawarden Park. This path, which is clear throughout, leads through the park and into Bilberry Wood. There are several diverging pathways, but these are not rights-of-way. There are also several sites of former mill industry, though little remains evident.

After crossing a stile, move up to walk alongside a wall and parallel with the course of an old streambed flanked by sycamore and hawthorn. When the wall ends, go forward over another stile into light, broadleaved woodland and follow a broad track to an offset cross track Ⓐ. Go half-left and cross into a continuing track (pond on the left) that soon leads out of the woodland and into the northern end of a hedged lane (Cherry Orchard Road).

On reaching Cherry Orchard Farm Cottage, the track becomes a surfaced lane and runs on pleasantly to a T-junction with an old B-road at Old Warren. Turn right (west) here, following the road steadily uphill and passing the **Spinning Wheel Tavern**, formerly known as the Old Hawarden Castle Inn, but which changed its name in the 1970s.

Higher up the lane, pass through a stile/gate combination onto the continuing but now unused road. Press on past a footbridge and now visibly (and acoustically) taking a parallel line with the A55. Eventually, further progress ends at another gate/stile Ⓑ at Stoney Hill. Through this turn right on a surfaced lane, passing Stoneyhill House, until the lane merges with another arriving from the left. Now cross a signed step-stile Ⓒ, and walk downfield towards a farm.

On reaching the farm and there crossing a stile beside a metal gate, bear to the right of an open, corrugated iron, barn to a stile giving onto the A550. Cross the road and turn right walking a short distance to a signed footpath on the left. Over this, follow a field edge with a hedgerow on the right to another stile in a field corner **D**. From here, a few strides lead onto Slack Road and the bridge over a railway line. Follow Slack Road, left, a short distance, before turning right into Ledsham Lane.

At the end of Ledsham Lane, the route enters the grounds of Higher House. Go forward to a clearly signed, enclosed path in the form of a hedged tunnel leading briefly up to a metal step-stile. Over the stile, bear right walking down the field edge beside a fence, and when this breaks away, bear half-left to another stile in a field corner and from this continue in the same direction over two pastures to a step-stile near Oaks Farm. Go forward to another stile giving onto a wide, hedged lane, flanked by a golf course. Keep on in the same direction, to pass beneath a railway bridge.

Immediately after the bridge, bear left on a descending track. Shortly, as the track bends to the left and starts to ascend, leave it for a footpath on the right going forward to a stile to the right of a metal gate, and then continue along a broad track. Follow this along the edge of the golf course which brings you via yet another stile onto a narrow path that leads up to the A550, with the starting car park in view to the left. ●

HAWARDEN ● 39

walk 13

Dyserth and Graig Fawr

Start: Dyserth, Denbighshire

Distance: 4½ miles (7km)

Height gain: 560 feet (170m)

Approximate time: 2½ hours

Route terrain: Surfaced railway trackbed, hilltop pasture, farm fields, minor roads

Parking: Anglia car park at start (next to Anglia Industrial Park)

OS maps: Landranger 116 (Denbigh & Colwyn Bay), Explorer 264 (Vale of Clwyd/Dyffryn Clwyd)

GPS waypoints:
- SJ 062 792
- Ⓐ SJ 060 806
- Ⓑ SJ 063 801
- Ⓒ SJ 073 791

This pleasing walk with far-reaching views begins along a section of a disused railway line originally built to serve the mines and quarries in the surrounding hillsides, extracting lead, zinc, limestone and silver. The route later climbs through National Trust woodland to the top of a local prominence before striking out to connect with Offa's Dyke Path on its final stretch northwards to the coast.

Leave the car park by taking to a broad surfaced track that soon becomes evidently a disused railway trackbed, the Prestatyn to Dyserth Way. The onward route is simple: follow the trackbed. This is flanked by several flower species typically associated with the harsh environment that accompanied railway lines: red campion, hawkweed, bloody cranesbill, oregano, hart's tongue fern and valerian among other limestone-loving plants that have established themselves here.

Continue as far as Y Shed Ⓐ, a craft hub, heritage centre and **café**. Leave the trackbed here, and branch right and immediately right again through a kissing-gate into the woodlands of Graig Fawr.

> **London and North Western Railway**
>
> Y Shed, close to the village of Meliden, was a goods shed on the branch line of the London and North Western Railway, known as the Prestatyn and Cwm Railway. The line was used mainly for minerals and goods, but did run a passenger service for a time, until 1930.

The ascending path, which curves round the northern slopes of Graig Fawr rises steadily. Just before reaching a metal kissing-gate, branch right (signpost) up a stepped path that rises steeply onto the top of the limestone hillock. When the steep ascent eases and the path divides, go left beneath overhead powerlines and soon break out into open hill pasture framed by bracken.

The summit of Graig Fawr rises to the right. So, follow the edge of the bracken to locate a broad path going right and shortly left that leads up to the trig pillar on the summit. From the summit retrace the outward steps, but instead of

0 200 400 600 800 METRES 1 KILOMETRES
MILES
0 200 400 600 YARDS ½

SCALE 1:25 000 or 2½ INCHES to 1 MILE 4CM to 1KM

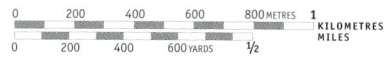

swinging round to head back for the powerlines, keep forward over a low hillock and then ahead across rough ground, flowered by mouse-eared hawkweed and ladies' bedstraw, to reach a lane opposite Mount House **B**.

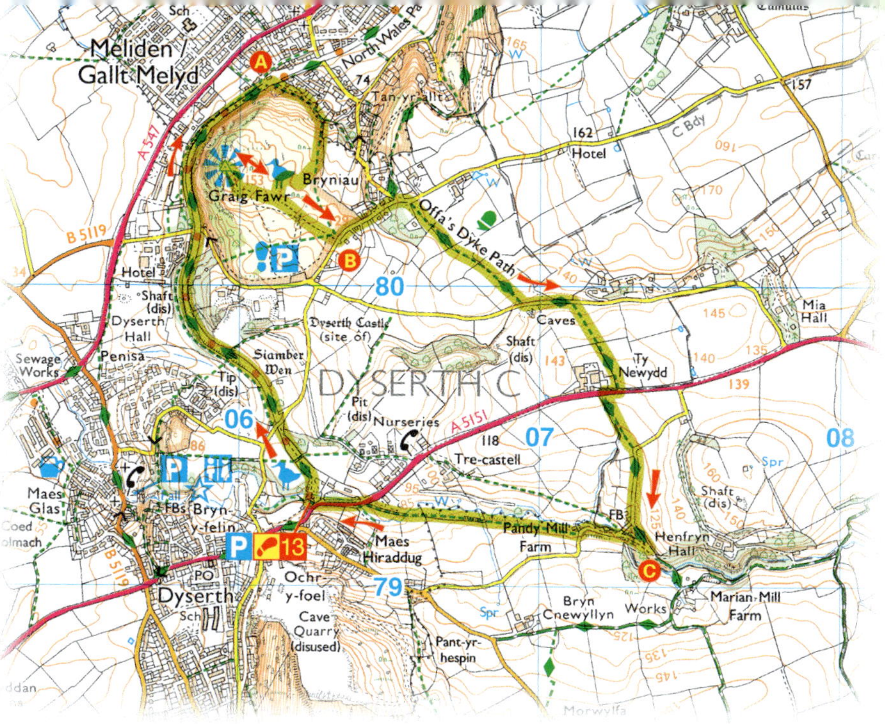

Turn left, and walk up the road, passing Castle Cottage, a reminder that Dyserth once had its own castle (SJ 060 798) a little to the south-west of the route. Just after passing a lane on the left, leave the road by crossing a stile near the entrance to Clarence House. The route here joins the southbound Offa's Dyke Path (signed 'Marian Cwm'), which it follows through several fields, finally to emerge on another narrow lane.

Turn left and walk as far as a kissing-gate on the right giving into a sloping pasture. Head up-field to locate another kissing-gate in a hedgerow, from which the path descends beside a fence to reach the A5151 near Ty Newydd farm.

Cross the A-road diagonally right, to pass through another gate just on the county boundary. Head downfield to tackle a step-stile giving onto a narrow lane, and turn right, following the lane until it makes an acute turning (right, **C**) and soon passing the remains of Grove Mill. Grove Mill was a flour mill, erected in 1815, the newest of four mills in this Marian Mills area.

Pass the mill, and continue until the lane makes a pronounced turn to the left at Grove Mill Cottage, leaving it through a gate giving into a short stretch of rough pasture. Go forward to another gate that accesses what will turn out to be an elongated stretch of scrub, seasonally overgrown, but through which the path is seldom in doubt.

The scrubby path eventually breaks free at a sloping pasture and a gate. Cross another narrow field and go forward below powerlines and along a broad track to emerge on the A5151. Turn left and cross the road to cover the short distance back to the start. ●

walk 14

Along the River Clwyd

Start
Rhyl (Marine Lake), Denbighshire

Distance
5½ miles (9km)

Height gain
70 feet (20m)

Approximate time
2½ hours

Route terrain
Surfaced riverside paths and gravel tracks; a little road walking

Parking
Car park at start (Pay and Display)

OS maps
Landranger 116 (Denbigh and Colwyn Bay), Explorer 264 (Vale of Clwyd/Dyffryn Clwyd)

GPS waypoints
- SH 996 806
- Ⓐ SJ 003 805
- Ⓑ SJ 006 801
- Ⓒ SJ 022 780

This largely flat and easy walk simply ambles along both sides of the Afon Clwyd between Rhyl and Rhuddlan, taking in the far-reaching views of the Clwydian Hills and the north-eastern summits of Snowdonia. The river flats and marshes are popular with a range of wetland birds, and a pair of binoculars may well enhance your day with a chance sighting of something rare.

This is a clockwise circuit, starting at a car park near Foryd Bridge, on the edge of the Marine Lake. Leave the car park at the riverside end, and turn left to walk along the top of an embankment, as far as a railway bridge. Here, dip left through trees into the grounds of the Marine Lake, which is encircled by a miniature railway track.

Rhyl

Rhyl has long been a popular holiday resort along the North Wales coast, with every imaginable amusement to keep visitors entertained. The place is largely a Victorian invention, and Marine Lake came about when Rhyl Urban District Council transformed a marsh at the mouth of the river, known as the 'Mudlands', into a boating lake. The site began to boom when Albert Barnes constructed a fun fair here (now no more) in 1910, which took pride of place for nearly 60 years. In 1895, Rhyl was an up-and-coming resort seeking to cash in on the Victorian seaside holidaying vogue. In 1845, Rhyl boasted some fine, smooth sands extending for several miles, and was a favourite resort for sea bathing frequented by numerous visitors for whom three 'respectable' hotels were established. Before 1826, Rhyl consisted only of a few scattered dwellings.

Go forward between the lake and the miniature railway line, and on the far side of the lake follow the railway line as it swings left, until you can leave the marine park by bearing right into a side street. At a crossroads, turn right and walk to, and over, a pedestrian footbridge spanning the main North Wales railway line Ⓐ. Immediately over the bridge, turn right, through a gate giving into Glan Morfa Community Woodland. Here the landscape has been transformed from a landfill rubbish tip into new woodland, a project started in 2006.

As soon as you pass through the gate, the ongoing path divides. Branch left and now follow the surfaced path as it loops around the edge of the embryonic woodland to meet an

inlet, where it is deflected inland. Continue as far as another path division **B**, and there turn right to cross the inlet (signed for Brickfields Pond).

Press on along the surfaced path, which soon heads back towards the river, and then follows it all the way to Rhuddlan. On the way you pass beneath the modern A525, and a short way further on reach the edge of Rhuddlan **C**.

Of particular note as you reach Rhuddlan is the imposing castle, one of 17 built by Edward I in his campaign to suppress the Welsh. Just beyond the castle is the only remaining part of its Norman predecessor, a mound called Twt Hill, built by William the Conqueror in 1073. A 'twt', or 'toot' hill is a primitive look-out post from which the surrounding countryside could be defensively observed, hence the expression to 'have a toot'.

As you reach the edge of Rhuddlan, turn right across a footbridge spanning the river, and continue beside the main road on the other side, as far as the turning into Marsh Road. Here, turn right, and now simply follow an almost arrow-straight lane and track past the Sun Valley Caravan Park and towards Rhyl, with lovely views across the marsh and its birdlife.

As you approach the railway line again, dip left to use a tunnel beneath it, and then walk out towards Foryd Bridge, beside which **The Harbour** pub is a convenient place for a little refreshment before crossing the road-bridge to complete the walk.

> **Statute of Rhuddlan**
>
> In the High Street of Rhuddlan, the Old Parliament House is said to be where Edward I enacted the Statute of Rhuddlan in 1284, which brought Wales fully under English administration and divided the country into counties on the English pattern.

ALONG THE RIVER CLWYD

walk 15

Cyrn-y-brain

Start
Ponderosa Café, Denbighshire

Distance
4¼ miles (7km)

Height gain
590 feet (180m)

Approximate time
2½ hours

Route terrain
Heather moorland and gravel access track

Parking
Car park at start, off A542, Horseshoe Pass, north of Llangollen

OS maps
Landranger 117 (Chester & Wrexham/Wrecsam), Explorer 256 (Wrexham/Wrecsam & Llangollen)

GPS waypoints
SJ 192 481
Ⓐ SJ 208 488
Ⓑ SJ 214 495

For all its simplicity, Cyrn-y-brain is not short of merit, having a spectacular view that on a clear day can have you believing you can see the whole of Wales. This modest summit, nonetheless a 'Marilyn' – for those who collect hill summits in box sets – is the highest point of the heather-blanketed Ruabon Moors, a Site of Special Scientific Interest. 'Heather' tends to be synonymous with 'grouse', and the moors are indeed managed for red grouse shooting, though parts of the moorland also provide a habitat for black grouse.

The route of ascent is straightforward, safe enough in mist and winter conditions. Begin from the large parking area across the road from the **Ponderosa Café**, and pass round to the right of the café. A grassy area at the rear hosts a small pond behind which a fence has two circular kissing-gates. Take the right-hand one of these (though either will do), and walk forward alongside a fenceline, through heather, until the path finally emerges on the gravel-surfaced track that serves the radio stations above.

Now simply turn right, and follow the track. There are a couple of diverging shortcuts, but while they may ease the underfoot surface, they don't add anything to the walk. It's the views that count here, and expansive they are extending north-west into Snowdonia and, if your imagination allows, as far south as the Brecon Beacons.

Close by the first wireless station compound a collapsed shelter-cairn to the left of the track Ⓐ marks the highest point of the route (1,853 feet/565m). From here a clear trail runs on,

Sir Watkin's Tower

There is some lack of clarity about who built the tower (and why). It was most likely one of the extensive Williams Wynn family of Wynnstay in Ruabon – one of the wealthiest families in Wales – who were responsible for developing the quality and diversity of the moors and producing several Members of Parliament. Certainly there is an associated claim that from the tower, which incidentally appears to have been built on top of a Bronze Age burial mound, the owner could see the five counties in which he held lands. For certain, the old Welsh counties of Caernarfonshire, Denbighshire, Flintshire, Merioneth and Montgomeryshire can be seen, along with Cheshire, Shropshire and Lancashire.

heading for the trig pillar and the remains of the so-called Sir Watkin's Tower that can be seen on the horizon. Pass another compound, beyond which the trail is intermittently boggy, but soon improving and arriving at a signpost **B** for the tower, reached by crossing a stile and walking on through heather.

Once having taken in the view, simply retrace your outward steps back to the Ponderosa.

On top of Cyrn-y-brain, looking across to Snowdonia

CYRN-Y-BRAIN • 45

Flower-filled pastures on Walk 19, from Llandegla

Slightly harder walks of 2½–3½ hours

Tremeirchion

walk 16

Start
Tremeirchion, Denbighshire

Distance
5 miles (8km)

Height gain
935 feet (285m)

Approximate time
2¾ hours

Route terrain
Hill farm fields, quiet lanes

Parking
Roadside parking at start (limited)

OS maps
Landranger 116 (Denbigh & Colwyn Bay), Explorer 264 (Vale of Clwyd/Dyffryn Clwyd)

GPS waypoints
- SJ 081 726
- Ⓐ SJ 085 735
- Ⓑ SJ 082 743
- Ⓒ SJ 089 740
- Ⓓ SJ 094 731
- Ⓔ SJ 098 723

The walk begins by a steady uphill walk along roads that lead to the village of Tremeirchion, and while roads feature at various times, most are quiet country lanes that connect glorious stretches of Clwydian countryside. Once on the high ground, the views are extensive and reach as far as the summits of Snowdonia (Eryri) with Tryfan and Moel Siabod especially prominent.

From the starting point, cross the road to walk up the B5429 (signed for Holywell). A steady pull leads to a branching lane on the right (also signed for Holywell) just as the gradient starts to ease. This leads up to Tremeirchion and the village church.

> **Tremeirchion**
> The village of Tremeirchion was formerly among the holdings of the Anglo-Welsh Salusbury family, and briefly attracted fame when dinosaur bones were found here. The church (Corpus Christi) is ancient and its churchyard boasts a yew tree estimated to be at least 800 years old. Close by is a 14th-century Celtic cross said to inspire miracles, though what miracles the cross caused to be performed is not recorded. The walk continues by heading north along the base of the Clwydian Range before climbing to meet and follow Offa's Dyke Path in a southward direction. Splendid views across the Vale of Clwyd accompany the walk throughout much of its length.

From the church, walk up the road past the **Salusbury Arms** as far as a footpath (kissing-gate) on the left giving onto an enclosed path. From the next gate, cross a field to a metal kissing-gate. Stride across the corner of the next field (following a stretch of the North Wales Pilgrim's Way), and then walk half-left towards the next gate and from this go half-right and descend to the far corner of the field Ⓐ.

Walk up and along the right-hand field edge, rising steadily. Over the top of the rise, move a little to the right to a waymark, and from this walk down alongside a hawthorn hedgerow on the right. In the field corner, look for a gate accessing a narrow neck of woodland. On leaving the woodland, turn left, and then

TREMEIRCHION • 47

The 'Miracle' Cross, Tremeirchion

walk out to meet a surfaced lane.

Turn right and walk up the lane, soon enclosed between high hedgerows. Go as far as a step-stile on the left and from this, cross to the right-hand field edge and walk along it towards a small copse. A step-stile in a corner accesses a narrow enclosure and having crossed another stile, go forward along a field edge and soon pass through a small patch of gorse.

On leaving the gorse, soon go left over a stile into woodland, through the cool embrace of which a narrow path leads out to arrive at a narrow lane. Turn right up this and walk as far as a distinct path on the right, Offa's Dyke Path **B**.

The path initially rises into woodland. Continue to a gate on the left and here continue with Offa's Dyke Path, which now rises gently across a hill slope. Go on to pass a perfectly placed bench with splendid views west over the Vale of Clwyd to the distant summits of Snowdonia (Eryri). From the next gate, go forward and soon target a field gate/kissing-gate **C** giving onto a tree-shaded track. Turn left and walk out to a surfaced lane. Turn right, descending, and continue to a T-junction. Turn left, briefly, and soon turn right onto another lane for Cefn Du and Sodom.

Go down the lane, continuing past the turning for Pen Uchaf, and go on, rising gently, until the lane bends to the left **D**. Here, cross a stile to the left of a field gate and then take to a broad grassy path ascending onto the slopes of Cefn Du. The path becomes less clear, but generally drift a little to the left (east) to target a step-stile over a fence. Beyond this maintain the same direction, rising gently to the top of Cefn Du and then in the general direction of a single wind turbine.

The route reaches a stile in a field corner and over this goes forward alongside a double fence to a kissing-gate close by the wind turbine. Descend on a narrow, shaded path through gorse, holly and sycamore that emerges onto a surfaced lane at a bend **E**. Immediately, turn right through a metal field gate and take to a wide and ancient track flanked by raised field boundaries and hawthorn. The ongoing track soon starts to descend as it curves round the headwaters of a tributary of the Afon Clwyd and runs on to a field gate, beyond which it continues through a wooded strip.

The track comes down to the end of a surfaced lane. Keep forward, following the lane until, just after it bends left, leave it by turning onto a concrete track on the right that leads to the Y Graig Nature Reserve and an area of Common Land. As the hard surface bends right towards a house, leave it, on the left, by taking to a narrow, hedged path, descending to the entrance to the nature reserve.

Through the gate, bear left, still descending through the reserve, eventually to arrive at a kissing-gate, beyond which the path divides. Keep forward onto a descending path to a gate at the edge of the nature reserve.

> **Y Graig Nature Reserve** The Y Graig Nature Reserve cloaks a limestone outcrop and encompasses a variety of habitats that are a haven for birdlife, butterflies and wildflowers including rock rose, dog violet, salad burnet, forget-me-not, thistle and saxifrage.

Keep descending and soon leave the reserve at a surfaced lane. Follow this left to a T-junction and turn right, now following the B5429 past **Beuno's Tea Room** and the entrance to Brynbella. For a while the lane has no footpath, but one soon materialises and leads back along the B-road to the starting point.

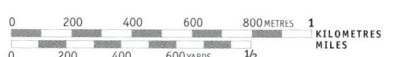

SCALE 1:25000 or 2½ INCHES to 1 MILE 4CM to 1KM

TREMEIRCHION • 49

walk 17

Ty Mawr and the Pontcysyllte Aqueduct

Start
Ty Mawr Country Park, Denbighshire

Distance
5½ miles (9km). Shorter version: 3 miles (4.8km)

Height gain
500 feet (150m)

Approximate time
2¾ hours

Route terrain
Farmland, riverside walking and canal towpath

Parking
Ty Mawr Country Park

OS maps
Landranger 117 (Chester & Wrexham/Wrecsam), Explorer 256 (Wrexham/Wrecsam & Llangollen)

GPS waypoints
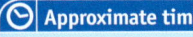 SJ 283 414
Ⓐ SJ 270 420
Ⓑ SJ 268 421
Ⓒ SJ 259 423
Ⓓ SJ 251 419
Ⓔ SJ 249 417
Ⓕ SJ 268 421

There is pleasant waterside walking to be had on this route, beside the River Dee as well as along the towpath of the Llangollen branch of the Shropshire Union Canal. But the most impressive feature of the route is the towering and dramatic Pontcysyllte Aqueduct, which carries the canal over the Dee valley. The walk climbs beside the aqueduct, but the shorter version omits most of the canalside walking.

Ty Mawr Country Park has excellent facilities for families, including tame animals and a variety of farm stock, and is an ideal place to start this largely level walk in the valley of the River Dee.

50 • WALK 17

🗒️ Put your back to the Visitor Centre entrance and turn left, walk along the right-edge of the tarred play area through a kissing-gate beside a gate at the far end. Turn right and go through a gate in a fence – there's a fingerpost here 'Country Park Walk and Aqueduct'. The surfaced path gradually descends and bends left, passing by donkey, goat and sheep enclosures.

Soon after the path levels out, turn right through a gate signed 'Footpath to Aqueduct'. Drop down the steps and follow the boardwalk through a copse to reach riverside meadows. The surfaced path skirts these above the Dee, with views ahead (when the trees are not in leaf) to the aqueduct. Beyond the wide concrete bridge, pass to the right of the pumping station and trace the path through to a point beneath Pontcysyllte Aqueduct.

Look for the steps on the right **A** immediately before the aqueduct and ascend these, pass under the last arch and walk up to a road. Turn right, cross a bridge over the canal by Trevor Basin and turn left on to the towpath, here joining Offa's Dyke Path. Turn left over the first footbridge and continue along the other bank of the canal.

At an Offa's Dyke Path fingerpost **F** *turn left for the shorter walk, picking up route directions from the next point at which* **F** *appears in the text.*

For the full walk turn right over the

Pontcysyllte Aqueduct
This was designed by the renowned canal engineers Thomas Telford and William Jessop and opened in 1805, carrying the Llangollen branch of the Shropshire Union Canal at a height of 127 feet (38m) above the River Dee. At over 1,000 feet (305m) in length it is one of the true engineering marvels of the Industrial Revolution, a giant technological leap for the time.

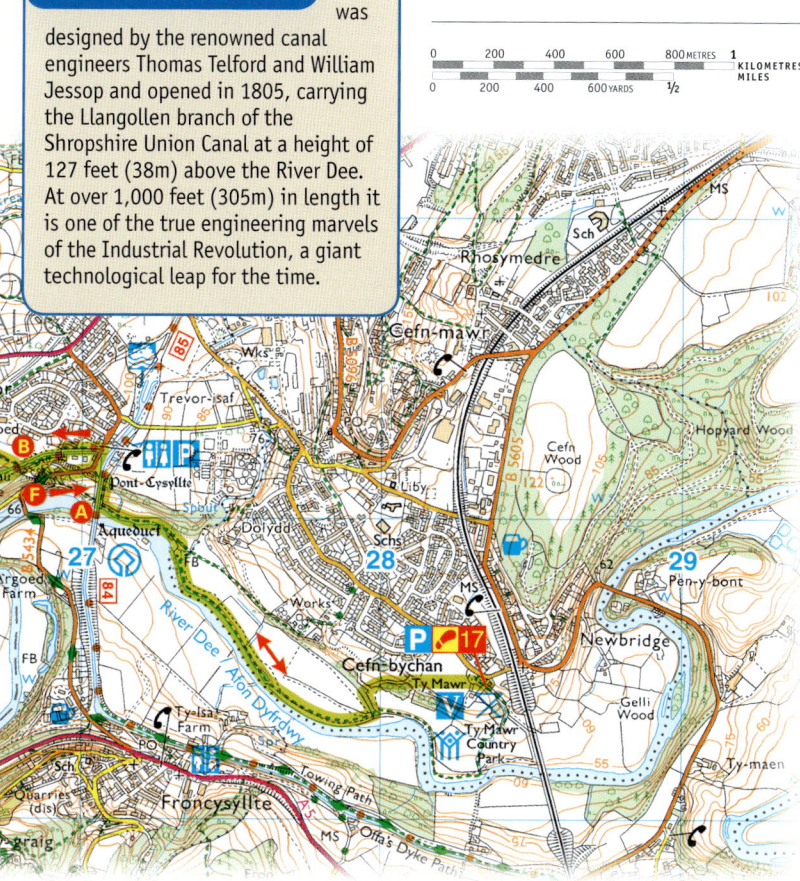

SCALE 1:25 000 or 2½ INCHES to 1 MILE 4CM to 1KM

TY MAWR AND THE PONTCYSYLLTE AQUEDUCT • 51

Boat on Pontcysyllte Aqueduct

next footbridge **B** bear left and head diagonally across a field to a kissing-gate. Climb it, turn left to walk below the embankment of a disused railway and the path bends right to pass through a tunnel. Turn right, follow the path to the left and continue along an enclosed tarmac path, climbing steps to a road. Turn left, cross the road and walk the pavement to reach, on your right, Trevor Hall Road. Turn along this and trace the quiet lane to a right-hand bend **C**. Here, fork left along the gravelled drive, signed as Offa's Dyke Path. Keep ahead on this as Offa's Dyke Path departs to the right; in the trees to your left is the little 18th century estate church.

Just before reaching Trevor Hall, turn left and climb a stile next to a field gate, then bear right down the descending track beside a fence on your left. Pass below the woods and bend left to a stile, then a second one and a third near a house, and walk ahead to the road. Turn right on the narrow pavement.

In 300 yards turn left along the lane **D** signed for **Bryn Howel Hotel**. Walk past the hotel driveway and on to a junction. Turn right along the roughening lane (there's a 'Low Bridge' restriction sign here) and walk to and across the canal bridge **E**.

Circle back-right underneath this bridge, putting the canal on your left and joining the tranquil, tree-lined towpath. There are pleasant views of the River Dee below and the surrounding hills, and later Pontcysyllte Aqueduct comes into sight again. At a metal bridge (No. 33) you briefly rejoin the outward route but at an Offa's Dyke Path fingerpost **F** bear right off the towpath and drop down the path to a driveway. Look half-right for a way-marked flight of steps leading down to a road. For a great view of the aqueduct and River Dee divert right down to a bridge (200 yards); otherwise turn left uphill and walk to the left-hand bend where a fingerpost directs you right, back onto the outward leg of the walk and the steps down beside the aqueduct. Simply retrace the route back to Ty Mawr Country Park, with the graceful railway viaduct as a background.

Prestatyn Hillside

walk

On this walk in the most northerly part of the Carneddau, there are extensive views over Prestatyn (which lies immediately below), Rhyl, the Vale of Clwyd and the North Wales coast. Most of the second half of the route uses first a disused railway track, and later a stretch of Offa's Dyke Path as it climbs above Bishopswood, which clothes the steep hillside.

Start	Prestatyn Hillside Viewpoint car park, ½ mile north of Gwaenysgor, Flintshire
Distance	5¼ miles (8.3km)
Height gain	760 feet (230m)
Approximate time	2¾ hours
Route terrain	Hill road walking and farmland pastures
Parking	Car park at start
OS maps	Landranger 116 (Denbigh & Colwyn Bay), Explorer 265 (Clwydian Range/ Bryniau Clwyd)
GPS waypoints	SJ 074 819
Ⓐ	SJ 075 810
Ⓑ	SJ 072 805
Ⓒ	SJ 062 800
Ⓓ	SJ 062 794
Ⓔ	SJ 065 809
Ⓕ	SJ 070 813

Start by turning right out of the car park and walking along the lane into the quiet village of Gwaenysgor. Pass a children's play area and immediately after a small church, turn right Ⓐ along a lane and a few yards after the lane becomes a rough track, take the fingerposted stone stile on the left immediately after the driveway for 'Tir Gwelyog', entering a wide grassy track.

Climb a wooden stile and then, at a bend, take the gate-side stone stile in the corner and turn right along the field edge to find another stile in a corner. Climb this and look half-left to sight a cottage. Aim for this climbing a stile and head for the field corner near the cottage, where a stile gives access to a lane Ⓑ. Turn right and remain on this lane for ¾ mile (1.2km).

Good views open out across the Vale of Clwyd and the prominent hill of Graig Fawr on your right. Keep left at a junction, remaining on the lane to reach another junction just before a National Trust car park Ⓒ. Here turn left along another lane and after 300 yards, turn right over a stile. Walk across a field, pass through a gate and keep along the top edge of a sloping field, heading gently downhill. At the bottom go through another gate, continue straight on, and then turn left along a rough track and shortly fork right along a wider track. In 50 yards, look on your right for a small wooden bridge leading to a metal kissing-gate, take this and walk through a belt of trees to the edge of a meadow. Bear half-right to find a kissing-gate in the corner. Use this and turn left with the fingerpost for the Prestatyn–Dyserth Way, descending a flight of wooden steps to gain the tarred trackbed of a former railway Ⓓ.

Turn right along this and go under the bridge. This was the old London and North Western Railway branch line from Prestatyn to Dyserth, and you remain on it for the next 1¼ miles (2km). Pass by the former goods shed at Meliden Station (Y Shed) and stay on the track to reach the end of housing on your left (there's also a golf tee here) **E**. Turn right, use the kissing-gate and rise up the steep pasture to another kissing-gate; beyond this walk up the steep tarred lane. This becomes a wooded track, passes through a kissing-gate and in a further 100 yards meets a junction with Offa's Dyke Path (ODP). Turn left; in a further 100 yards turn left again with the fingerpost for Prestatyn Hillside and ODP, climbing gently through Bishopswood (Coed yr Esgob), once owned by the bishops of St Asaph.

The path becomes fenced above an old quarry then rises to a three-way fingerpost, here bear right on ODP, pass through a wall gap and then rise increasingly steeply through gorse and scrub. The path levels, offering superb views off to your left to the distant

Graig Fawr cutting, Meliden

horizon of Snowdonia's peaks, and then descends to pass right of a fenced mine-shaft before rising again through a thicket. Emerging from this, you'll soon reach an old fingerpost and a stile on your right ⓕ. Climb the stile (marked as Gwaenysgor) and walk ahead along the foot of the slope towards the distant village. The path enters low woodland before reaching a kissing-gate, beyond which trace the hedged path to a walled old village well on your right. On your left here, climb the few steps, use the stile and walk ahead to another one, then stick to the right-hand side of the pasture to reach a stile into a lane. Turn left to return to the car park. ●

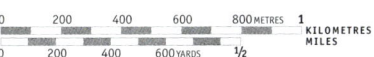

SCALE 1:25 000 or 2½ INCHES to 1 MILE 4CM to 1KM

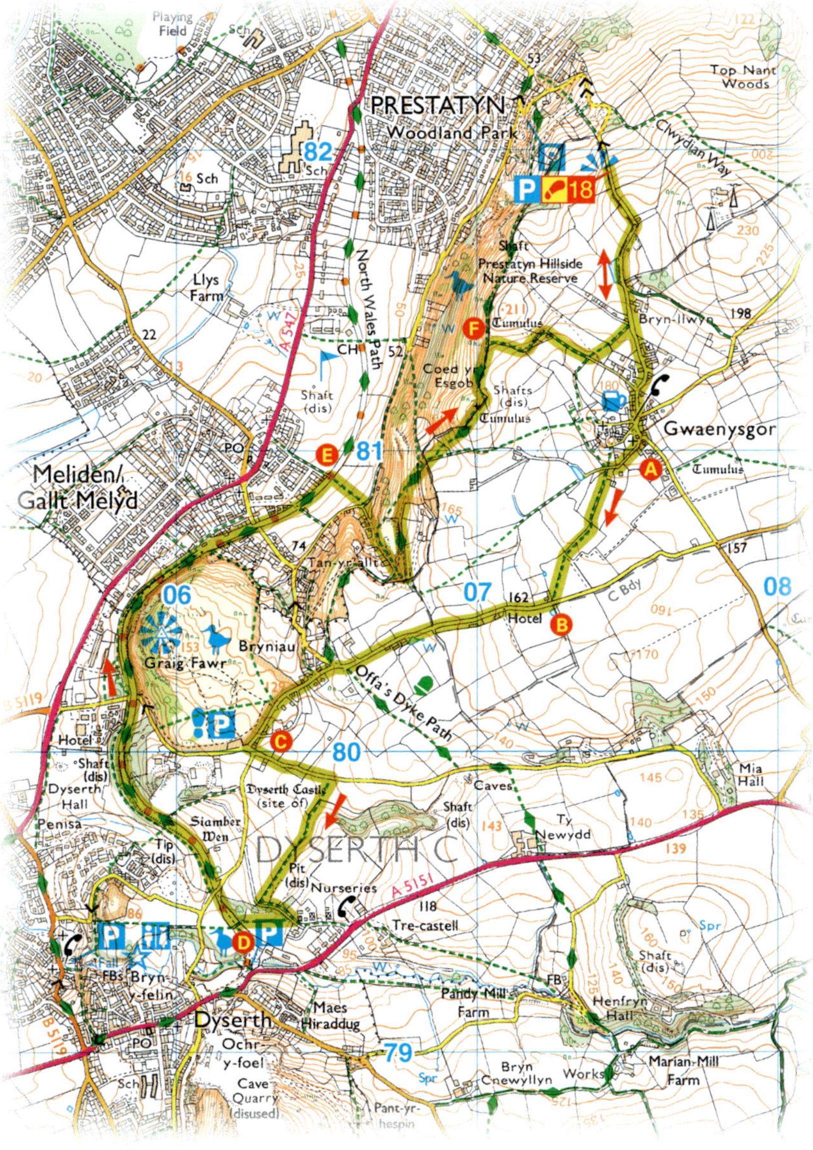

PRESTATYN HILLSIDE ● 55

walk 19

Llandegla and Moel y Waun

Start
Llandegla, Denbighshire

Distance
5½ miles (8.7km)

Height gain
705 feet (215m)

Approximate time
3 hours

Route terrain
Field paths and minor roads

Parking
At start (community car park)

OS maps
Landranger 117 (Chester & Wrexham/Wrecsam), Explorer 256 (Wrexham/Wrecsam & Llangollen)

GPS waypoints
- SJ 196 523
- Ⓐ SJ 194 529
- Ⓑ SJ 189 535
- Ⓒ SJ 180 537
- Ⓓ SJ 171 533

The small village of Llandegla, with a convenient (and welcome) shop and café, is located along one of the ancient drove roads of North Wales in the upper valley of the River Alyn. This agreeable walk saunters away from the village, making use of what is now Offa's Dyke Path for the first half of the walk. The opportunity is taken to visit the outlying summit of Moel y Waun before returning to Llandegla on quiet lanes. There are many step-stiles throughout the walk.

Leave the car park and head towards the church, taking the lane to the right of it (signed for Prestatyn, the northern terminus of Offa's Dyke Path), and soon branch off onto a descending track and down through a metal gate. Continue on a narrow path (which does not accord with the line of the Offa's Dyke Path as shown on mapping), soon sandwiched between the softly murmuring slimline River Alyn and a fence. Eventually the route arrives at a footbridge Ⓐ spanning the river. Cross the bridge and on the other side bear right along the edge of a large undulating pasture, finally bidding farewell to the river for the moment.

Shortly the track rises to the remnants of a field boundary and dyke, which may be part of the original Offa's Dyke. Here, bear right to pass through a kissing-gate into a sloping pasture, and keep on in the same direction now with a fence on the left to another gate giving once more onto a short stretch of the ancient dyke. Walk

Fan-shaped ridges What becomes more evident as the route gains height is that the rock formations along Offa's Dyke Path form a series of fan-shaped ridges from south-west to north-east, caused by an ancient fault in the bedrock. Most of the ridges are now topped with trees and the alignments are clearly seen, both in the mapping to the north-west of Llandegla and visually as the walk progresses.

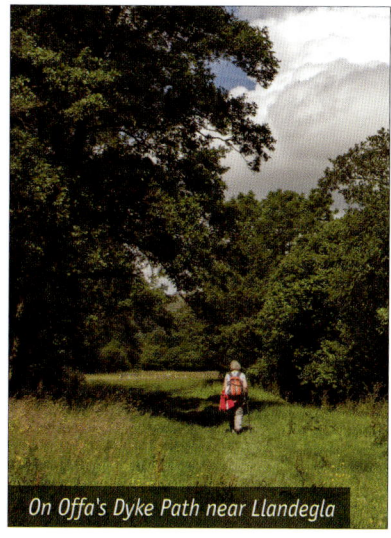

On Offa's Dyke Path near Llandegla

alongside a fence to a waymark pole, and from there go forward to another gate and footbridge. Go ahead on a clear path, with a stream to the right that soon departs.

Pass through a wooden gate and turn left briefly, and then right (at two large rocks) to walk along a hedged boundary featuring, in places, several elm trees. At the far side of the pasture, pass through another wooden gate onto an enclosed path that leads up past an interesting rock feature on the left **B**, where limestone rocks have been tilted

SCALE 1:25 000 or 2½ INCHES to 1 MILE *4CM to 1KM*

0 200 400 600 800 METRES 1 KILOMETRES

0 200 400 600 YARDS ½ MILES

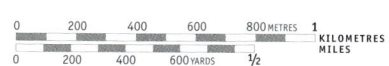

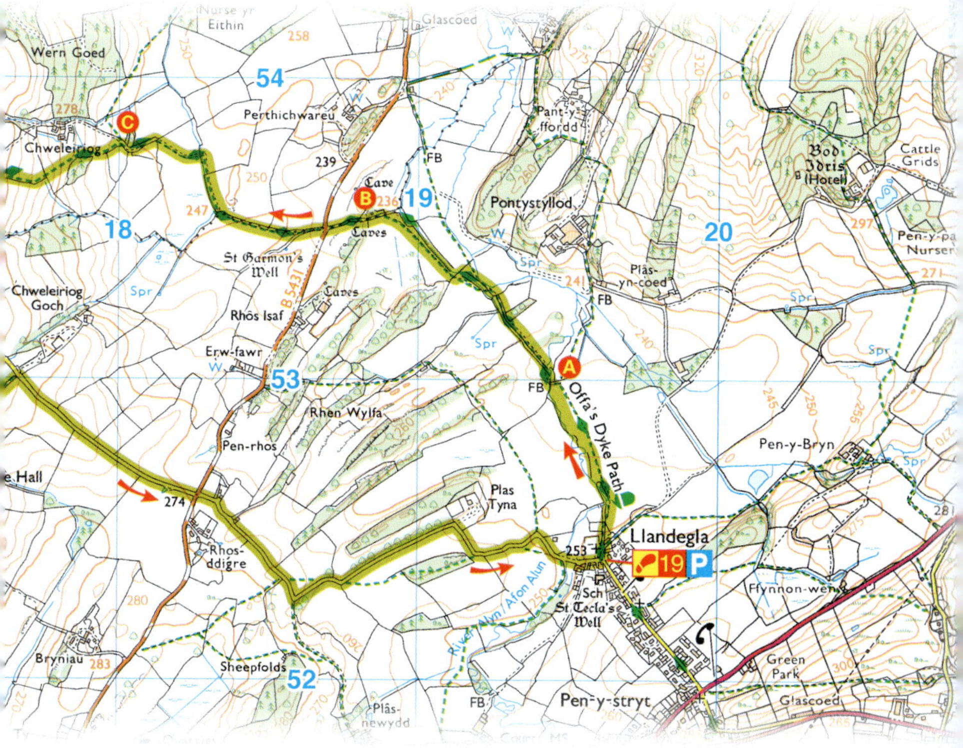

upright by earth movements several million years ago. Not always evident, but this is the site of an ancient spring that would have issued palatable water and may, like others in the area, have been regarded as a holy well.

The path leads onward to a surfaced lane (B5431). Cross to the track opposite that leads up to Chweleiriog Lwyd Farm. Shortly, the track begins to rise gently before descending just as easily to cross a cattle-grid and take a dog-leg line towards the farm. Just as the ongoing track becomes surfaced **C**, leave it by bearing left onto a grassy path at the foot of a sloping pasture that is the first of several following stile/pasture combinations that pursue a clear route to pass Tyddyn-tlodion and emerge onto a narrow lane.

Anyone seeking to return to Llandegla need only turn left here and follow the lane back to the village, crossing the B5431 en route.

Turn right and head up the lane until it levels and you can leave it at a signed path on the left. Go forward briefly to then parallel the curving course of a turf dyke, rising steadily on to it and passing a gnarled and bent tree determined to live on. The hillside here is blanketed in gorse, and when an open stretch appears on the right, maintain the same direction (south) following the ancient boundary, the course of which is clearly visible, marked out by more gorse and a couple of impressive beech trees.

Follow the raised mound of the dyke to a step-stile and gate and keep forward until directly above a farm (Brenhinlle Fawr), and close by a wooden field gate **D** the route starts to descend. From here, if including Moel y Waun, strike upwards (west)

across steadily rising slopes to a fence-line giving onto Open Access Land and the ridge then eases up to the summit. Retrace your steps to **D**.

Continue descending on a path that heads towards a small area of woodland above a farm, round which the route has been diverted (right) on a clear trod to a stile and gate. Beyond, press on, always descending towards a narrow elongated strip of woodland rising onto the hillside to the right, and eventually arriving at a couple of field gates at Accre Hall. Once through the gates turn sharply left and follow the access lane out to the minor road encountered earlier in the walk.

At the T-junction turn right and now follow this lane, crossing the B5431 along the way, back to Llandegla. Although subsequently there are a couple of clear opportunities to shortcut some of the road walking by paths across pastures, the lanes are generally quiet and rejoice in a kaleidoscope of wildflower colour: purple bird vetch, lilac field scabious, yellow agrimony, the gold of honeysuckle and the blue of speedwell and selfheal.

The lane returns to Llandegla, re-crossing the River Alyn and passing St Tecla's Church, an early-medieval structure recorded in the 13th century as a chapelry of Valle Crucis Abbey (Walk 2).

Llandegla village centre

Chirk and the River Ceiriog

After an attractive walk across the parkland surrounding Chirk Castle, with fine views of the great border fortress, the route joins the Offa's Dyke Path and drops into the lovely Ceiriog valley. It then climbs, and continues along the south side of the valley before descending again to the river. The final stretch keeps by the Ceiriog, crossing delightful meadows and passing beneath the adjacent 19th-century viaduct and the 18th-century aqueduct, built to carry different forms of transport across the valley and both engineering triumphs of their respective eras.

Note that this route can only be walked between 1 April and 30 September as part of it, between **B** and **C**, uses a National Trust permissive path which is open only between those dates.

Start at the crossroads in village centre by the medieval church and turn along Church Street. Take the first turning on the left, by the war memorial, keep ahead over first a railway bridge, and then over the canal, and turn right **A** at a public footpath sign. Follow the path ahead through the woods, keeping to the left-hand path and looking for a wooden hand-gate down to the left in 200 yards. Use this and walk up the sloping field to another hand-gate into a lane.

Cross into the entry **B** virtually opposite and take a hand-gate beside a field gate. *This is the start of the permissive path through Chirk Park, open only between 1 April and 30 September. It is well marked by large, white-tipped posts.* Keep to the left edge of the field to use another hand-gate beside a field gate, from which head half-right across the parkland to use a hand-gate through a fence. Turn left, shortly use another hand-gate (not the one on your left) and soon join the line of the inner state wall on your left. Drift right to find a stile onto the main castle drive at a T-Junction. Go ahead along the road towards the car park.

Keep right at the fork into the car park. Stay alongside the left edge of the car park to the very end at a cattle-grid, here taking the first of a series of hand-gates beside field gates, all marked by white-tipped posts. Simply remain along the left edge of the pastures to reach a tarred lane at a bend.

walk 20

Start
Chirk, Wrexham

Distance
5¾ miles (9.2km)

Height gain
975 feet (295m)

Approximate time
3 hours

Route terrain
Parkland, farmland and meadows

Parking
Car park near start

OS maps
Landranger 126 (Shrewsbury & Oswestry/Croesoswallt), Explorer 240 (Oswestry/Croesoswallt) and 256 (Wrexham/Wrecsam & Llangollen)

GPS waypoints
- SJ 291 376
- **A** SJ 283 377
- **B** SJ 281 378
- **C** SJ 263 389
- **D** SJ 264 374
- **E** SJ 267 370
- **F** SJ 280 371
- **G** SJ 290 372

The viaduct and aqueduct at Chirk

Immediately past the lodge house **C** on your left, turn left through a kissing-gate, joining the Offa's Dyke Path (marked by an acorn logo). Trace the field road to and past a redundant stile and ahead to a ridge-top kissing-gate. Continue ahead along the right edge of the woodland to a stile beside a metal gate. Beyond this the path steepens, dropping to a kissing-gate into a rough lane. All the while there are fine views down into the Ceiriog valley. Turn left down this lane, which becomes tarred at a farm. Remain on it to reach a junction above some cottages. Here turn left and trace the lane all the way to the main road. Take the lane opposite (entering Shropshire here), cross the bridge over the River Ceiriog and rise steeply to a T-junction.

Turn left **D** and remain on the lane for about ½ mile (800m) to a left-bend immediately past an old school **E**. Turn left here down the old lane marked by multiple waymark discs. This gives out between a cottage and a barn; keep ahead here through two close-spaced gates and along the grassy path to a kissing-gate. Through it bear right to reach a stile into the Woodland Trust's Pentre Wood. Climb this and join the path; in 150 yards climb the flight of steps on your right, then remain on the path as it soon drops back down more steps and comes close to the River Ceiriog, eventually to leave the woods and enter a meadow. Stick with the path close to the riverside trees; this eventually becomes a wider track and rises to a stile beside a gate at the foot of a rake of cottages. Turn left to a T-junction and left again to cross Pont-faen bridge.

Turn right through a kissing-gate **F** into the field immediately beyond the bridge and pick up the path that roughly follows the riverbank. Ahead, two multi-arched structures march across the valley. The nearest is a 19th-century railway viaduct; the farthest is Thomas Telford's aqueduct carrying the Llangollen branch of the

Shropshire Union Canal across the valley, impressive but not as amazing as his Pontcysyllte Aqueduct across the River Dee just a couple of miles (3km) away (see Walk 17). Use the kissing-gate and hand-gate beneath the structures and walk ahead, shortly bending left up a fenced track to find a gate onto the road near Chirk Bridge G. Cross over, bear slightly left through a metal gate, at a public footpath sign, and walk along a track. Where it curves to the right, keep ahead along an enclosed path, climb a stile, turn right over a ditch and then turn left alongside it. Bear right to head uphill along a grassy path, climb a stile, and turn right along a road to return to the start.

Chirk Castle Early on in the walk there are impressive views of Chirk Castle, completed in 1310, but regularly altered and modernised over the centuries. Unlike most of the other border fortresses, it has been continuously occupied since it was built, mostly by the Myddleton family. It is now a National Trust property and its elegant state rooms and formal gardens are well worth a visit.

SCALE 1:25000 or 2½ INCHES to 1 MILE *4CM to 1KM*

0 200 400 600 800 METRES 1 KILOMETRES
0 200 400 600 YARDS ½ MILES

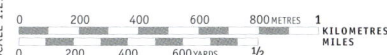

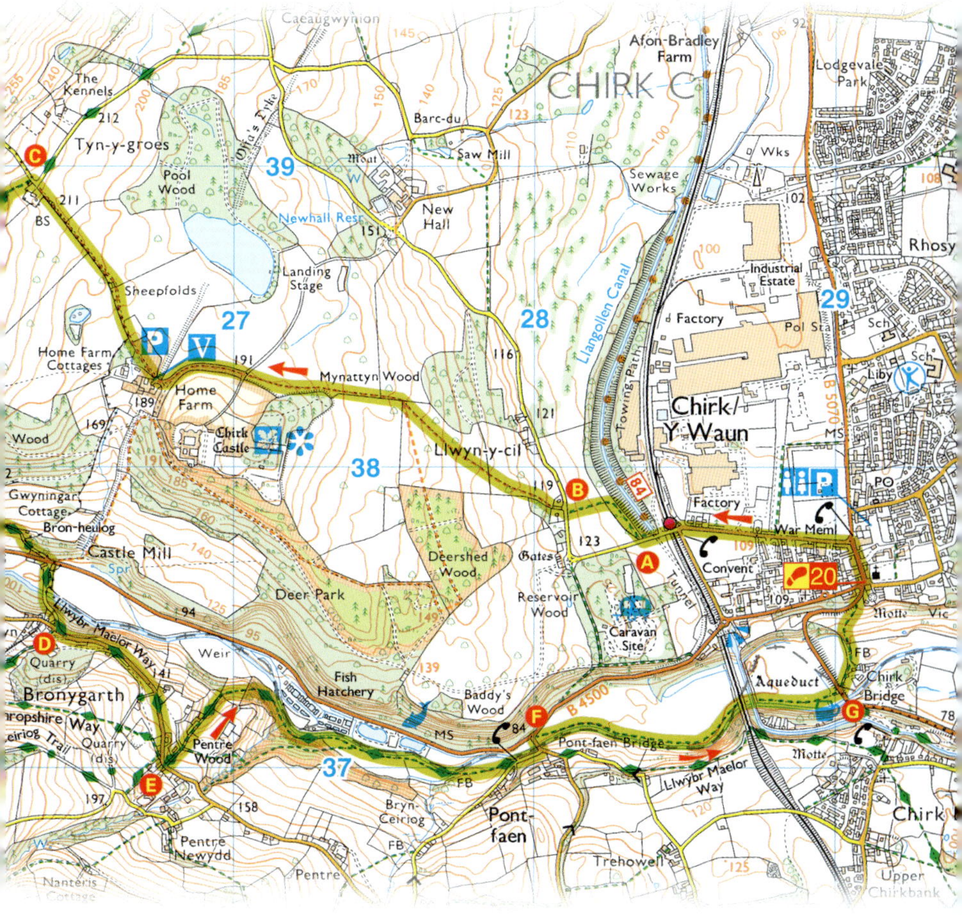

walk 21

Moel Famau

Start
Moel Famau woodland car park, Denbighshire

Distance
5¼ miles (8.25km)

Height gain
1,265 feet (385m)

Approximate time
3 hours

Route terrain
Woodland, open heather moorland

Parking
Car park at start (Honesty box, and Pay and Display)

OS maps
Landranger 116 (Denbigh and Colwyn Bay), Explorer 265 (Clwydian Range/ Bryniau Clwyd)

GPS waypoints
- SJ 172 611
- Ⓐ SJ 162 605
- Ⓑ SJ 161 626
- Ⓒ SJ 168 616
- Ⓓ SJ 163 615

Moel Famau is the highest hill in the Clwydian Range, on the border between Denbighshire and Flintshire. The hill, gives its name to the Moel Famau Country Park, and has been central to the Clwydian Range and Dee Valley Area of Outstanding Natural Beauty since 1985, and, for hill baggers, is classed as a Marilyn.

The walk has two distinct parts, beginning and finishing through woodland and plantations, but with a fine stretch of the Offa's Dyke Path between the two, an interlude that offers fine, far-reaching views of the Denbigh moorlands and the distant mountains of Snowdonia.

Start from the car park by walking out to the road, and turning right, up towards Bwlch Penbarras. After about 250 yards, leave the road by bearing left onto a wide forest trail, known locally as the Mushroom Path. This is a gentle start, rising gradually at an easy angle to the large car park at the pass Ⓐ; bear right to the road.

Cross the road, keeping left, and start up the broad track that is now the Offa's Dyke Path (signposted for 'Jubilee Tower'). When the track forks, keep left along the lower path, a delightful terraced path flanked by gorse. Views of undulating, rolling hills appear beyond the Clwyd valley and the towns of Ruthin, with its ancient castle/hotel, and Denbigh. To the south, Foel Fenlli is prominent, and, like Bron-y-felin to the west, was the site of an Iron Age hillfort. The walking is gentle and invigorating, easing steadily upwards in easy stages with numerous benches on which to rest, to a final pull to the Jubilee Tower that crowns the top of Moel Famau Ⓑ.

> **Jubilee Tower**
> The tower was built in 1810 to commemorate the Golden Jubilee of George III, and was designed like a three-tiered Egyptian obelisk. However, the tower was never completed because of a lack of funds. In 1862, a storm brought down the incomplete tower, following which the remaining upper part of the structure was demolished for safety reasons leaving just the base, the alcoves of which provide shelter from all but the most persistent winds.

Leaving the summit of Moel Famau can be problematical in poor visibility. A trig pillar stands forlornly nearby and beyond it a gate giving onto heather moorland. Ignore this direction,

0 200 400 600 800 METRES 1 KILOMETRES

0 200 400 600 YARDS 1/2 MILES

SCALE 1:25 000 or 2½ INCHES to 1 MILE 4CM to 1KM

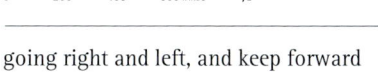

but look for another gate a little more to the south-east (to the right of the trig pillar), and through this soon engage a steep, shaly path descending quickly to the shelter of the plantation below.

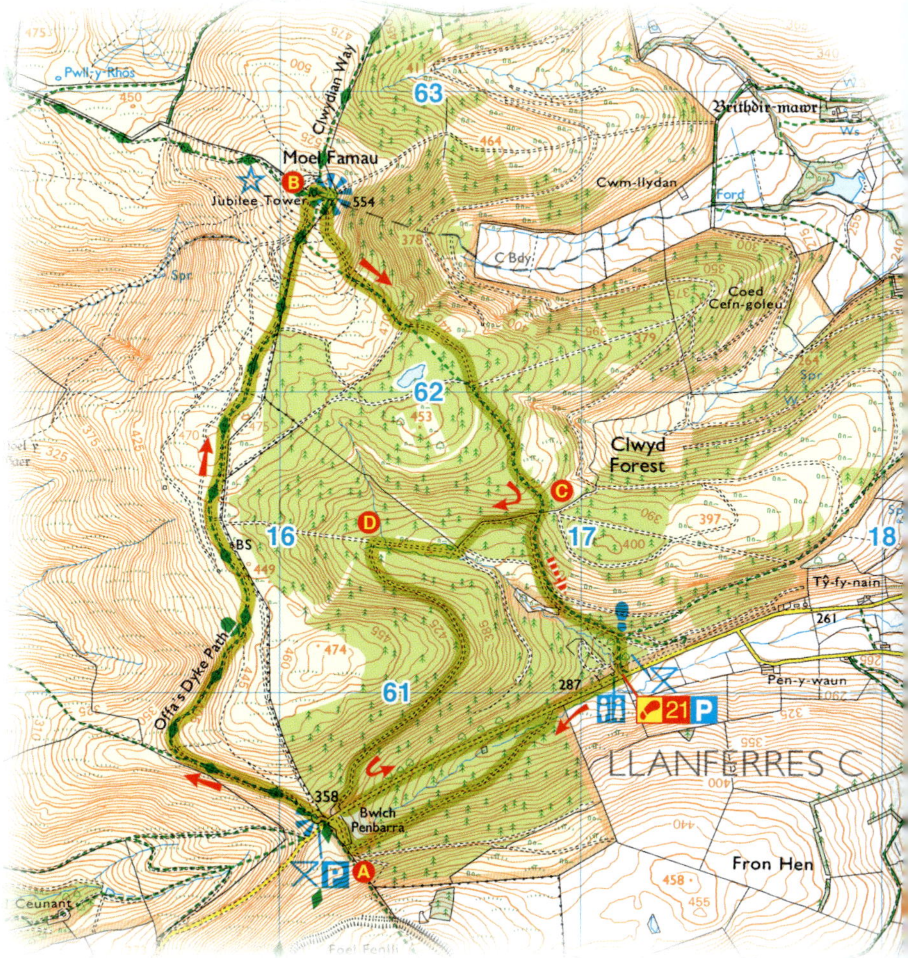

Press on down through the plantation, once more steeply, to reach a waymark post at a path junction **C**. *From here, by continuing to descend, you will be led directly back to the car park, should it be necessary to abbreviate the walk.* At the waymark, turn right (blue waymark with white spot), descending on a narrow path to reach a track junction, with trails going in a number of directions. Ignore trails going right and left, and keep forward on a broad track, initially open, that swings slightly to the right. Follow this for about 250 yards, and when the track divides **D**, bear left (white waymark).

The track curves round through the upper reaches of the plantation, and eventually drops easily towards Bwlch Penbarras. Just before reaching the road, swing acutely left through a gate and onto a descending gravel path that, ignoring branching paths, leads all the way back down to the start.

walk 22

Loggerheads and Cilcain

Start
Loggerheads Country Park, Denbighshire

Distance
6½ miles (10.5km)

Height gain
890 feet (270m)

Approximate time
3 hours

Route terrain
Woodland, farmland, some minor roads

Parking
Car park at start

OS maps
Landranger 117 (Chester & Wrexham/Wrecsam), Explorer 265 (Clwydian Range/Bryniau Clwyd)

GPS waypoints
- SJ 197 626
- Ⓐ SJ 189 637
- Ⓑ SJ 177 649
- Ⓒ SJ 171 647
- Ⓓ SJ 168 644
- Ⓔ SJ 183 634

The 80-acre (32-ha) Loggerheads Country Park centres around a beautiful wooded river valley, backed by dramatic cliffs and limestone outcrops; this is great for a short walk and as good a place as any to begin an exploration of the Clwydian Range. You soon realise that this was formerly an important lead mining area, and evidence of this industrial legacy will be encountered in a few places as you wander through the woodland.

The walk begins in the company of the River Alyn (Afon Alun), which has a surprising connection with the German composer, Felix Mendelssohn. He is known to have stayed at nearby Coed Du Hall, at Rhydymwyn, as a guest of John Taylor, a mining engineer and entrepreneur, and the third of his three Fantasies for piano ('The Rivulet': Opus 16, No. 3), composed as gifts for Taylor's daughters Anne, Susan and Honora, evokes the River Alyn, where Mendelssohn and the girls sometimes stopped to rest during walks and horseback rides.

From the car park, head towards the visitor centre, shop and **café**, continuing past them to cross a bridge over the river. Turn left, below the impressive limestone cliffs of Pen y Clogwyn. The path leads on through pleasant woodland, following the true right bank of the river.

At a track junction (signpost), keep to the path for Cilcain and the Devil's Gorge. Keep on to pass an isolated property (cattery and kennels) and go forward on the Leete Path. A broad vehicle track leads on into an ascending surfaced lane, at which point, cross to a woodland path opposite Ⓐ.

When the path divides at a waymark, keep to the lower path, and press on in due course to pass the impressive gash that is the Devil's Gorge. Remain on the continuing Leete Path, now high above the river and at various times at the base of limestone cliffs. Follow the path until eventually it emerges onto a road. Turn left, descending to cross a road bridge spanning the Alyn.

Now, follow the road, ignore branching footpaths, and climb briskly until the road swings sharply to the right, and here leave it on the apex, at a wooden footpath sign (for Pentre and Cilcain). Walk up to a stile, and beyond, continue along the left edge of a paddock to another stile. Press on, at the edge of a steep slope down to a tributary of the Alyn, to a third stile and a level path beyond.

At a stile, where the path divides again, keep forward for Pentre, still remaining throughout above the slope

0 200 400 600 800 METRES 1 KILOMETRES
0 200 400 600 YARDS ½ MILES

SCALE 1:25 000 or 2½ INCHES to 1 MILE *4CM to 1KM*

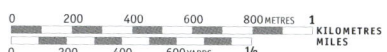

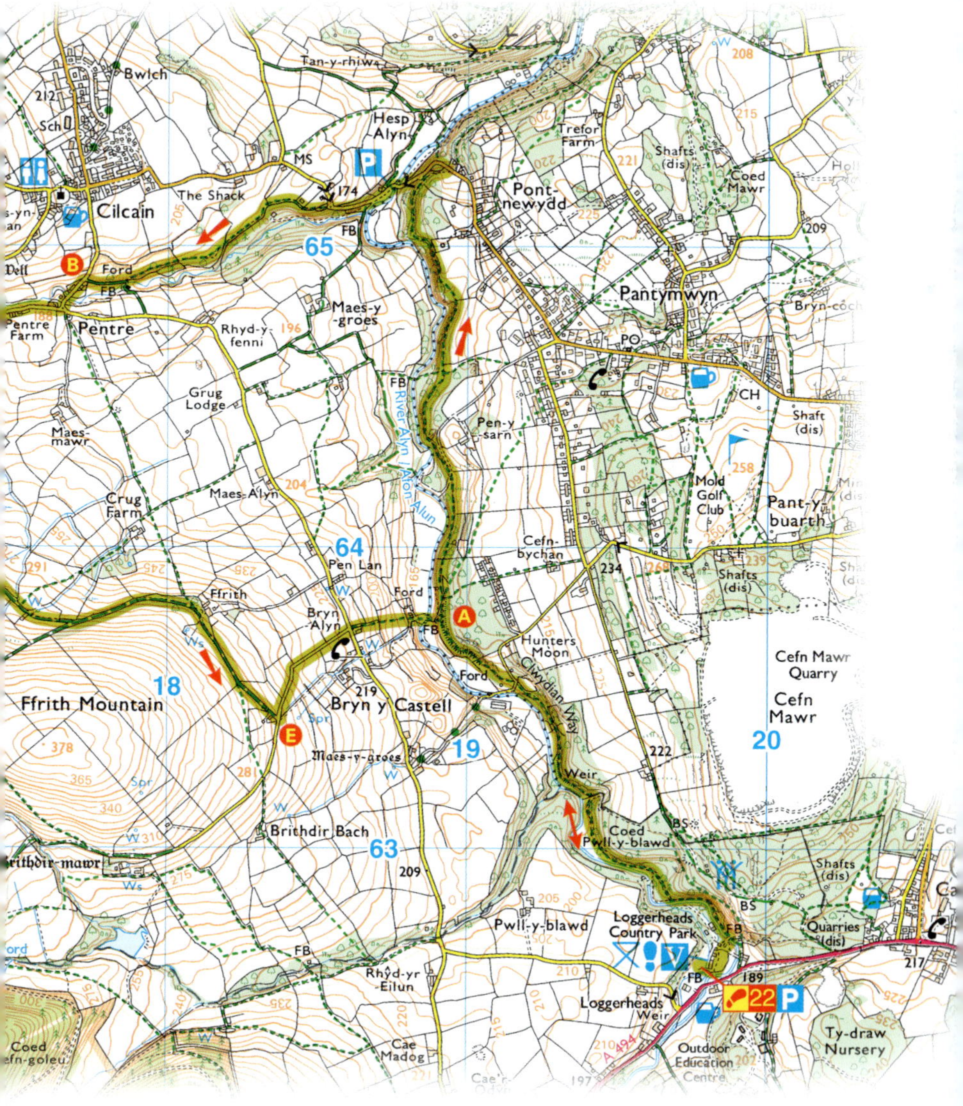

The viaduct and aqueduct at Chirk

down to the river. At the next path junction, again at a signpost, keep left for Pentre-Cilcain, now along a narrow path above the river. The path descends to a point close by a narrow footbridge. Ignore the bridge, and instead bear right on an ascending sunken path up to a surfaced lane **B**.

Anyone wanting to visit the **White Horse** pub in Cilcain, should turn right here, staying on the lane, then turning left at each junction to pass the pub, and, later, rejoin the main route **C**.

Otherwise, turn left, descending past Wayside Cottage. Follow the lane downwards, and then, as it climbs and swings to the left, leave it by branching right onto a much narrower lane, passing Cross Foxes Farm, and leading to a road junction at which the lane from Cilcain is met **C**. Here, leave the lane by going forward and then immediately left through a gate onto a rough farm track. Within a few strides, leave the track by crossing a high stone stile on the right, and then go forward along the left-hand field edge, and maintain the same direction across fields until the route emerges via a stile in the far left corner of a field, onto a broad track, near a track junction **D**.

Turn left onto a broad track, soon cross a shallow ford and go through a bridlegate, and climb up to another gate, there keeping forward alongside a fence. Cross a section of boardwalk and onto a gently rising path below a line of ancient hawthorn. Keep forward past a farm and out along a vehicle track.

On the way, you pass a brick structure on the right. This was a small decoy site, built during the Second World War to protect the valley water works.

Keep following the track until it emerges onto a narrow lane **E**. Here, turn left, descending to a T-junction. Cross the road, and onto an enclosed footpath that leads steeply down via stiles to a footbridge spanning the River Alyn. Over the bridge, tackle an awkward little ascent on the right, across limestone (slippery when wet), and, at the top, turn right to retrace the outward route back to the Loggerheads car park. ●

Setting off across the boardwalks for Moel Sych

Longer walks of 4 hours and over

walk 23

Penycloddiau and Moel Arthur

Start
Coed Llangwyfan, Denbighshire

Distance
7½ miles (12km)

Height gain
1,675 feet (510m)

Approximate time
4¼ hours

Route terrain
Heather and mountain moorland

Parking
Coed Llangwyfan car park: 1 mile (1.6km) east of Llangwyfan village

OS maps
Landranger 116 (Denbigh and Colwyn Bay), Explorer 265 (Clwydian Range/ Bryniau Clwyd)

GPS waypoints
- SJ 139 667
- Ⓐ SJ 121 689
- Ⓑ SJ 130 664
- Ⓒ SJ 140 656
- Ⓓ SJ 147 657

The first and last parts of the route involve two ascents and descents as you follow Offa's Dyke Path along the ridge of the Clwydian Hills, passing the prehistoric hillforts of Penycloddiau and Moel Arthur. The remainder is along clearly defined and generally flat tracks that contour along the side of the hills, making for easy, attractive and trouble-free walking. There are some pleasant wooded stretches and continuously fine views across the broad Vale of Clwyd.

Begin by going through a gate; at the fork in front take the right-hand track and at the next fork a few strides ahead, take the right-hand, uphill path, following Offa's Dyke Path waymarks. The path runs parallel to the track and heads uphill, steeply at times, along the right edge of conifers to a stile.

Turn right over the stile, here crossing the outer earthworks of Penycloddiau, an Iron Age hillfort, and continue uphill across the middle of the fort. After passing a cairn, you reach the outer defences again and at this point the views from this ridge top track, to the right and left and ahead along the undulating Clwydian Range, are of rolling hills and far, purpled heather moorlands. Bear right for a few yards and then turn left to continue across moorland, descending to a stile. Climb it, cross a low rise and then continue gradually downhill on the wide path, following Offa's Dyke Path waymarks to another stile Ⓐ just beyond a stand of pine trees.

Iron Age hillforts

The Penycloddiau hillfort is the largest on the Clwydian Range encircling 52 acres (21 hectares) making it one of the largest such Iron Age sites in Wales. There are a series of concentric earthworks, alternating defensive ditches and ramparts around a central enclosure where archaeologists have excavated evidence of roundhouses and ponds. Stone tools found at the site date back to the Bronze Age.

Moel Arthur has a much smaller, circular hillfort, 5 acres (2 hectares) in extent, crowning its summit. However, the ditches and ramparts are respectively among the deepest and tallest of any in Wales. There is an earlier Bronze Age tumulus in the centre of the hillfort. Three copper axes dating from the Bronze Age were found in 1962.

by the edge of attractive woodland, and with agreeable views across the Vale of Clwyd all the time. Finally the track bears left and keeps below conifers to reach a lane **B**.

Bear left, follow the lane round a right-hand bend and where it bends to the left, turn right at a public bridleway sign, along a track. This is another curving, partially wooded track that you follow through several more gates and from which there are again superb views over the Vale to be enjoyed. After 1¾ miles (2.8km), you go through a metal gate on to a lane **C**, turn left and follow the lane as far as Moel Arthur car park **D**.

Near the far end of the car park use

On the shoulder of Moel Arthur

Do not climb this stile, but turn left on to a broad track by a wire fence on the right. Keep along this winding track for the next 2½ miles (4km), passing through several gates, and at one stage

A pleasant track in the Clwydian Hills

the gap in the wall on the left, indicated by a fingerpost 'Offa's Dyke Path & Llangwyfan Wood,' and join a steepening path that curls through bracken and heather around the eastern flank of Moel Arthur. As the path levels, a short diversion can be made (left) to explore this fine Iron Age hillfort.

To reach the finish line, simply remain on the well-used Offa's Dyke Path, descending steadily via three stiles to gain a lane just a few paces downhill from the car park.

Moel Arthur from Penycloddiau

walk 24

Llantysilio Mountain

Start
Ponderosa Café, Denbighshire

Distance
7½ miles (12km)

Height gain
1,855 feet (565m)

Approximate time
4½ hours

Route terrain
Heather moorland; farmland; road walking

Parking
Roadside parking area, opposite the café

OS maps
Landranger 116 (Denbigh and Colwyn Bay), Explorer 256 (Wrexham/Wrecsam & Llangollen)

GPS waypoints
- SJ 192 481
- Ⓐ SJ 180 472
- Ⓑ SJ 171 465
- Ⓒ SJ 149 451
- Ⓓ SJ 149 460
- Ⓔ SJ 151 463
- Ⓕ SJ 168 475
- Ⓖ SJ 171 476
- Ⓗ SJ 174 478

There is little scope for losing one's way on this high-level traverse of Llantysilio Mountain: the track is a wide, gravel blaze through heather moorland, clear enough to follow on a moonlit night. But while the route enjoys clarity and far-reaching views, there is a surprisingly extended series of ups and downs that will call for numerous view-appreciating halts.

From the roadside car park opposite the **Ponderosa Café** a number of wide, grassy paths rise through the heather, climbing round and above a large quarry; that which heads towards the quarry and then passes to the left around it is the most direct route to the top of Moel y Faen.

Take the ongoing track as it descends, steeply in places, to a broad bwlch (pass) Ⓐ and then climbs steadily to the highest

point on the route, Moel y Gamelin, a neat summit crowned by a large cairn of rocks.

Another steep descent leads to a cross-mountain route **B** used by the Clwydian Way, from where you ascend once more, first to Moel y Gaer, and then up to the trig pillar on Moel Morfydd.

Follow the track down from Moel Morfydd, to intercept a lane **C**. Turn right, with fine views on your left over lush farmland, and walk gently up to Bwlch y Groes. Continue down the road as far as a signed bridleway on the right **D**, and here leave the lane for a lovely grassy trail flanked by heather, bracken, bilberry, intermittent gorse and myriad wildflowers.

Moel Morfydd

The view is splendid, reaching as far as Winter Hill in Lancashire, and across to the heart of Snowdonia, with Tryfan easily discernible, along with the Glyders, the Carneddau and the Snowdon massif. To the south the tops of the Berwyn Hills poke above intervening heights, while all around heather cloaks the entire hillside, a stunning sight in August and September.

There is evidence for human activity on these hills dating back to at least the Bronze Age, with a large burial cairn on the summit of Moel y Gamelin. Later, during the Iron Age, Moel y Gaer was chosen as the site for a small hillfort. In more recent times these rounded, heathery hills were transformed by extensive slate quarrying, mostly around the Horseshoe Pass, although with smaller quarries dotted around the hillsides. Many quarrymen lived in Rhewl and Llantysilio, walking the hillside tracks to the quarries each day.

Beautiful springtime sunshine over the lower slopes of Llantysilio Mountain

SCALE 1:25 000 or 2½ INCHES to 1 MILE 4CM to 1KM

0 200 400 600 800 METRES 1 KILOMETRES
0 200 400 600 YARDS ½ MILES

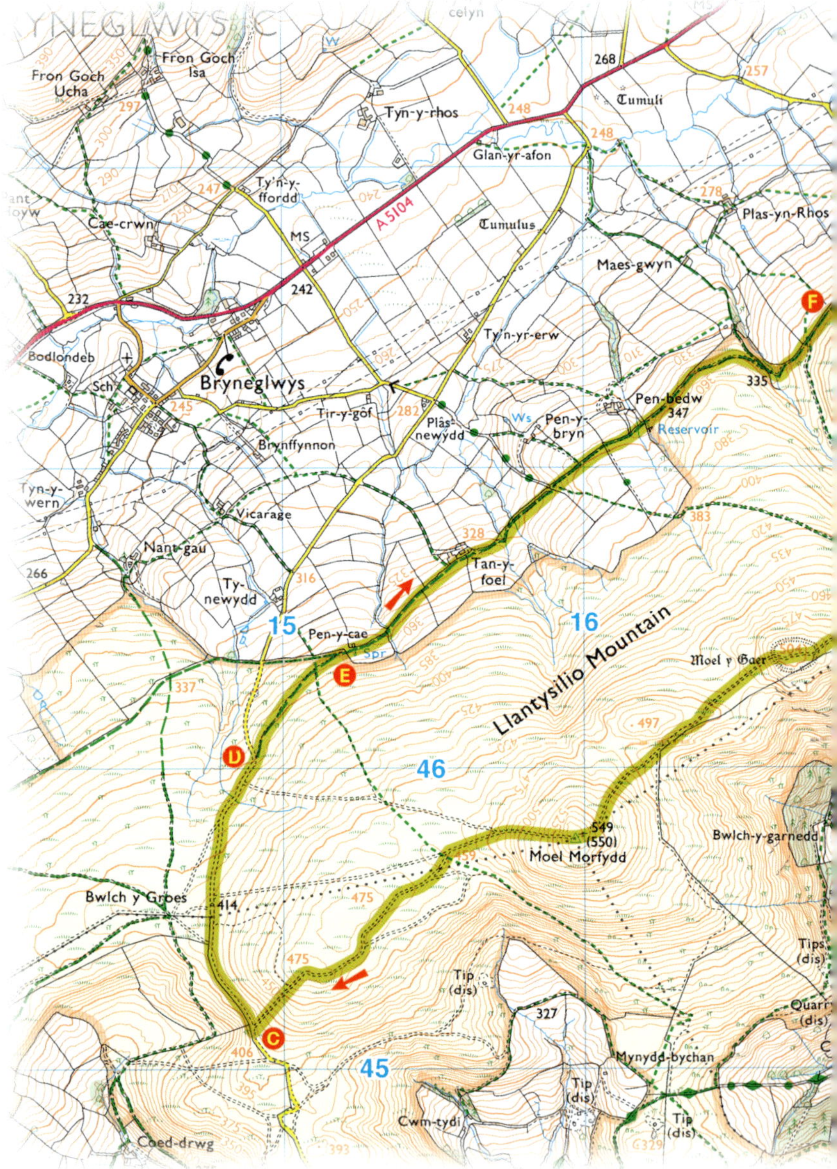

Follow the bridleway across the hill slope to intercept another bridleway running beside an intake fence. Close by, pass through a gate/stile **E**, and then continue across rough pasture to another gate/stile, beyond which a grassy path runs beside a fence and past Tan-y-foel farm. Press on, following the bridleway across numerous pastures, always roughly parallel with a fence on the left.

The path continues easily across heather moorland, accompanied either by a fence or a wall. When the wall and the ongoing bridleway diverge **F**, stay

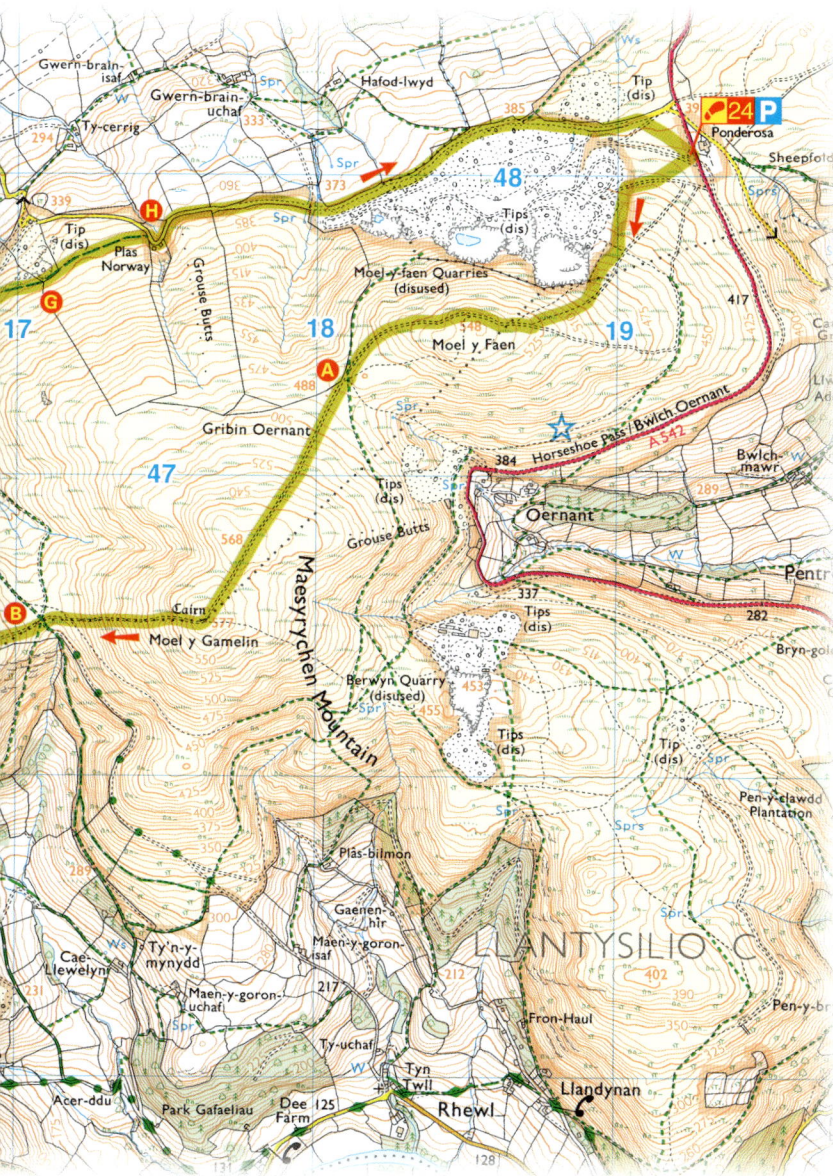

with the latter to meet a fence above the top edge of a quarry G. Here, the onward route lies over a fence and directly above the quarry, but a safer option keeps a little more distant from the quarry boundary. Both ways involve striding over a low fence, and then pressing on towards the concealed cottage at Plas Norway. The bridleway underfoot steers you towards the cottage, but you will need to move left to locate a gate H giving onto a narrow lane.

Turn right, up the lane, passing Plas Norway, and then simply follow the lane, past the Moel-y-faen quarries back towards the Ponderosa; the final section of the lane can be shortcut by a clear path through heather.

walk 25

Llyn Brenig

Start
Llyn Brenig visitor centre, Conwy

Distance
9 miles (14.5km)

Height gain
950 feet (290m)

Approximate time
4½ hours

Route terrain
Farmland, forest, lakeside paths and some road walking

Parking
Car park at start

OS maps
Landranger 116 (Denbigh and Colwyn Bay), Explorer 264 (Vale of Clwyd/Dyffryn Clwyd)

GPS waypoints
- SH 967 546
- **A** SH 966 543
- **B** SH 978 540
- **C** SH 983 574
- **D** SH 985 579
- **E** SH 971 581
- **F** SH 961 571

Llyn Brenig is situated amid the forests and rolling moorlands of Mynydd Hiraethog. This clear and well-waymarked circuit of the reservoir, which mainly uses a mixture of lakeside paths and tracks and forest roads, goes across meadows, over heathery moorland and through the conifer woods of Clocaenog Forest. Although a lengthy walk, the terrain is generally flat and easy, with the likelihood of a few muddy stretches, and there is a succession of fine views across the lake.

Llyn Brenig A centre for a whole range of outdoor recreation activities including walking, cycling, fishing, kayaking, sailing and water zorbing, as well as picnicking and bird watching, the 2,500 acres (1,000 hectares) of forest, moorland and lake at Llyn Brenig provide valuable wildlife habitats. The lake's star attraction in recent years has been the osprey pair that arrives in April on their return migration from Africa. Nest cameras relay pictures to the visitor centre, where there is an osprey exhibition supported by North Wales Wildlife Trust, who also have a viewing area and bird hide (limited entry, fee payable) for closer observation of the ospreys. The visitor centre, on the south-west corner of the reservoir, has a café and shop.

In summer, sand martins nest in large colonies along the shore of the reservoir (completed in 1976), and great crested grebe and goosander can be seen on the lake. The moorland comprises upland heath and blanket bog and has characteristic plants such as sphagnum moss, bogbean and cranberry, and is home to black grouse, curlew and skylark.

Stand facing the lake in front of the visitor centre and turn right, shortly using a hand-gate just above the jetty. This gate is marked with a Clwydian Way disc and also a cream 'walker' disc – these will become familiar as the walk progresses. Walk through to the western end of the stone-clad dam **A** and join the rough road across it.

At the far end **B** turn left, shortly going through a gate. Walk on to a gate and cattle-grid at the edge of the trees, remaining on the rough road through the woods and beyond around a series of inlets. Hairpin sharp left on the main track (there's an isolated old cottage off to the right) and continue above the reservoir. About 150 yards before reaching a gate, notice the low, circular stone structure on your left. This is a

Fishing a quiet corner of Llyn Brenig

ring cairn dating from about 4,000 years ago, and used, it is thought, for funerary rituals. Nearby is a distinct mound – this is Boncyn Arian burial barrow dating from much the same time. Use the stile **C** beside the gate and go ahead beside the car park to join a gently rising tarred lane. You're now at the edge of the Gors-Maen-Llwyd Nature Reserve – there's a bird hide along a path off to your left.

At the top of an incline **D**, look on the left behind a rough lay-by for a waymarked post, here picking up a well-walked path across the moorland. This soon curves round the edge of a wooded area and comes to roughly parallel the main road. There are regular Clwydian Way (CW) posts, although the path is hard to lose.

You'll reach a small, isolated stand of tall ash and short oak trees. Pass immediately left of these and follow the path to a CW post 100 yards beyond. From here, look ahead to espy a line of blue posts; you should take the very narrow path up past these, leaving the main path to curve away left. There are occasional low wooden steps on this path; eventually you'll reach a larger wooden post with a cream 'walker' disc on. Turn right here and walk the heathery path to reach another such post virtually at the roadside fence **E**.

Turn left along the wider, stony path that develops into a track, swinging away from the road and then coming close-by again. There are CW and 'walker' discs confirming the way.

Near a cattle-grid, the path angles away from the road one final time, shortly reaching a hand-gate giving access to this part of Clocaenog Forest. Keep ahead along the forestry road, which shortly becomes tarred. Cross the solid stone bridge over the Afon Brenig and rise to a crossroads **F**.

Turn left here with the tarred road, remaining on this as it weaves alongside inlets and along promontories to a junction and a 'No Entry' road sign. Keep ahead here, passing the sailing club to return to the visitor centre car park.

> **Gwylfa Hiraethog**
>
> Way off to your right, and well beyond the serried ranks of trees forming Alwen Forest, you should be able to pick out the gaunt, hilltop ruins of Gwylfa Hiraethog. This, 'The Wooden Palace', was built in 1908 as a shooting lodge by the wealthy Lord Davenport, and was claimed (somewhat disingenuously) to be the highest inhabited building in Britain at that time.

Red kite

LLYN BRENIG 79

walk 26

Point of Ayr and the Wales Coast Path

Start
Point of Ayr, Talacre, Flintshire

Distance
9 miles (14.5km)

Height gain
215 feet (65m)

Approximate time
4 hours

Route terrain
Sand dunes and coastal promenade

Parking
Choice of car parks at Talacre

OS maps
Landranger 116 (Denbigh & Colwyn Bay), Explorers 264 (Vale of Clwyd/Dyffryn Clwyd) and 265 (Clwydian Range/Bryniau Clwyd)

GPS waypoints
- SJ 124 847
- Ⓐ SJ 094 843
- Ⓑ SJ 061 838
- Ⓒ SH 996 808

This linear walk (well served by public transport) offers impressive seaward landscapes interspersed with quiet zones wherein lie several interesting wildlife inhabitants. In essence you do as much or as little as you wish; there are a number of points where you can opt out – maybe to explore Prestatyn or Rhyl, or just sit on the sands and let the world go by. Walk 14 can be joined at the end, and Walk 18 from Prestatyn. This is very much a free range walk, and in summer months likely to be busy with holidaymakers. The Point of Ayr is the northernmost part of the Welsh mainland and the coastal scenery features saltmarsh, sandy beaches and sand dunes.

From any of the car parks, head towards the beach. No sooner do you reach it and the Point of Ayr lighthouse (SJ 120 852) comes into view. This is a Grade II listed building, built in 1776 on oak foundations. It used to have two lights, one marking the mouth of the Dee estuary and the other pointing out to sea.

1 Map continues on p83

80 • WALK 26

Heading west, the route enters the Talacre Warren and Gronant Dunes, a Site of Special Scientific Interest and a Special Area of Conservation for good reason – this is a habitat of the sand lizard and the only breeding site in Wales of the natterjack toad.

Here, you have the choice of following one of several designated paths through the dunes or simply

Point of Ayr lighthouse

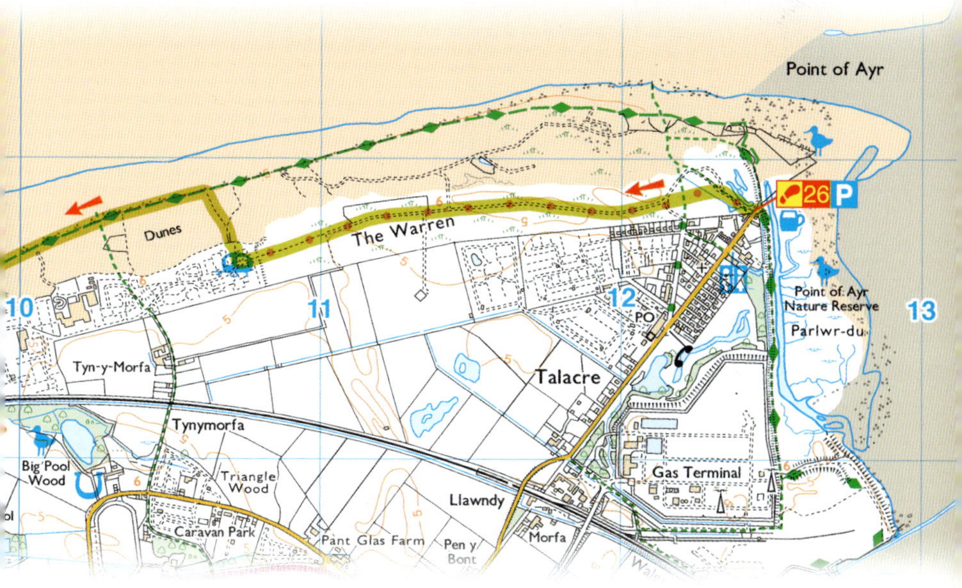

POINT OF AYR AND THE WALES COAST PATH ● 81

2 Map continues at the bottom of p83

The Begining and the End
sculpture, Prestatyn

The Dunes

The dunes are of some interest and you may encounter remnants of concrete lookout posts and pillboxes dating from the Second World War. This was a time when many families from the greater Liverpool region sought to evade bombing raids by seeking shelter among the Gronant dunes, living in shanty shacks or caravans. The seaward view no longer holds the threat of invasion, but is pinned in place by a host of wind turbines.

taking to the beach.

The route is following the Wales Coast Path, crossing from Flintshire into Denbighshire **A** as it heads for the Presthaven Sands Holiday Park. Once beyond the entrance to the holiday park, the path heads back seaward, along the beach, and soon passing a golf course to access the promenade that links Prestatyn and Rhyl.

Beyond a car park and approaching the Nova Centre, you come up against a remarkable sculpture **B** – the so-called 'Beginning and End' sculpture where you reach the northern end of Offa's Dyke Path. In the form of a stylised sun set on limestone blocks, the sculpture is the point from which you can head south for 177 miles (285km) to the Sedbury Cliffs, near Chepstow.

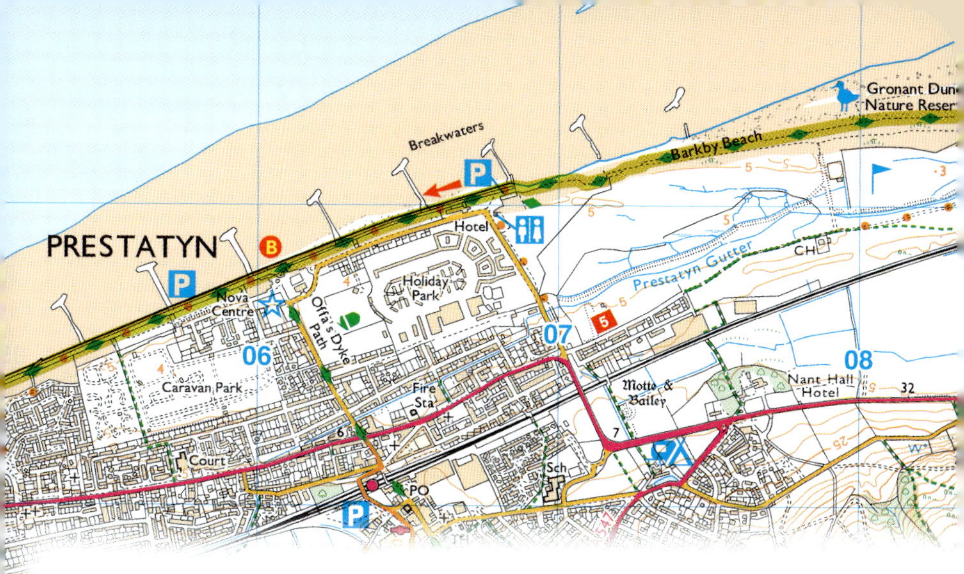

From here the route is simply a matter of following the promenade all the way to Rhyl, and maybe, in the right low-tide conditions, see something of the prehistoric forest that once occupied where the beach is today. The walk ends at a stunning bridge, Pont y Ddraig C, which opens vertically.

Bus services depart from Rhyl Bus Station for the 30-minute journey back to Talacre.

0 200 400 600 800 METRES 1 KILOMETRES
0 200 400 600 YARDS ½ MILES

SCALE 1:25 000 or 2½ INCHES to 1 MILE *4CM to 1KM*

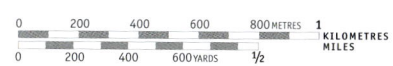

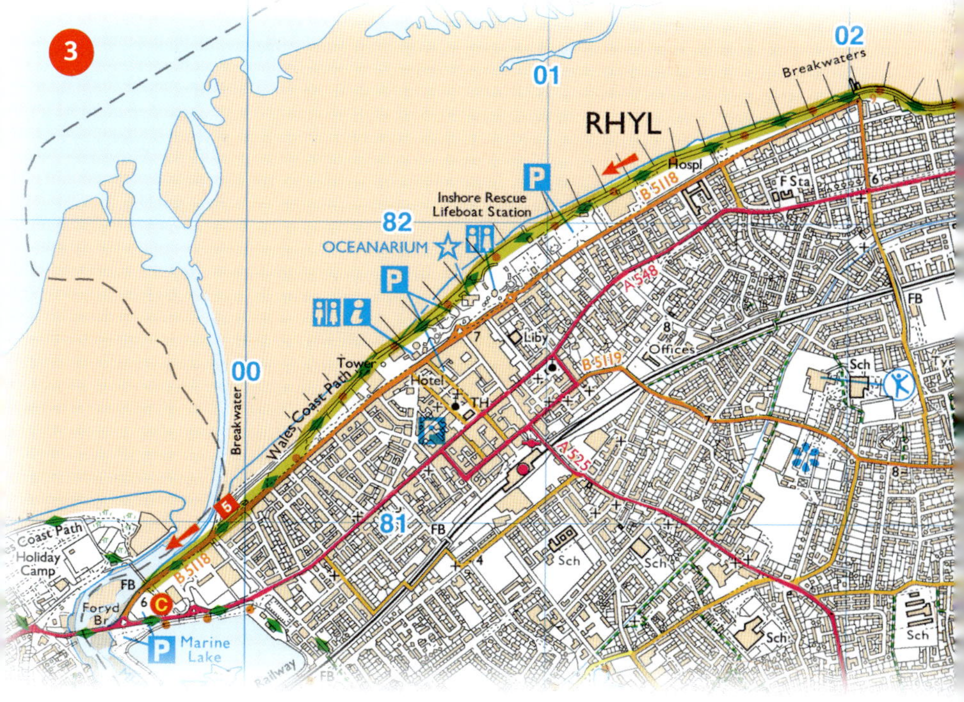

walk 27

Bwlch Maen Gwynedd and Cadair Bronwen

Start
Llandrillo, Denbighshire

Distance
8½ miles (13.6km)

Height gain
2,265 feet (690m)

Approximate time
5 hours

Route terrain
Mountain moorland and farmland

Parking
Car park at start

OS maps
Landranger 125 (Y Bala & Lake Vyrnwy/Llyn Efyrnwy), Explorer 255 (Llangollen & Berwyn)

GPS waypoints
- SJ 035 371
- Ⓐ SJ 037 369
- Ⓑ SJ 042 352
- Ⓒ SJ 076 340
- Ⓓ SJ 051 375

The walk leads through austere and remote terrain, into the heart of the Berwyn Mountains, to Bwlch Maen Gwynedd, a gap in the ridge linking Cadair Bronwen and Cadair Berwyn. Bwlch Maen Gwynedd itself is at 2,342 feet (714m), and from it the views along the ridge and down into adjacent valleys, are inspirational.

⚠ On the outward route some path sections are indistinct but improving, and you need to avoid a boggy area. The return uses a much clearer and easier track, but the entire route involves rough walking across mountain moorland and hillside, and should not be attempted in poor visibility, unless you are an experienced hill walker able to navigate competently.

Llandrillo is attractively situated on the Afon Ceidiog, a tributary of the River Dee, and from the bridge there is a fine view of the tower and spire of the church rising above the village.

From the car park entrance turn left along the main road. Cross to the village hall (Y Ganolfan) and take the waymarked path passing to the right of the building. Cross a stile and walk along an enclosed path, and shortly keep ahead along the right-hand edge of a field. From an offset hedge corner and oak tree, look left to locate a stile and fingerpost next to a field gate; join a lane here Ⓐ.

Turn right along the lane, go through a gate and start a gradual climb, passing to the left of Llechwedd farmhouse and up a green track to a field gate at the foot of woodland. Join the track beyond this, skirting the woods and passing through another gate. At a junction bear left, taking a wooden gate and rising along the track to a fork. Keep left here; the track steepens before emerging from the woods at a sharp left bend. On the right here are two gates; take the lower one and follow the old sunken lane as it rises gradually towards the high moors.

Go through a gate Ⓑ and, a few paces farther on, climb a stone stile beside a gate at the border of Open Access country – there's also a bridleway signpost for Craig Berwyn here and a National Nature Reserve board for Y Berwyn Reserve. Walk

Moel Ty-uchaf stone circle

ahead on the declining track, with a wall on your right. The next half mile (800m) or so may be waterlogged in places. The track descends towards a stream (Clochnant); at this stage it is important to bear left away from the stream in order to avoid a marshy area ahead, Gwern Wynodl.

Aim for the higher, drier, heathery moorland to the left, later bearing right back towards the stream and making for the distinct landmark of a small, rectangular conifer wood clearly seen ahead. Head towards it, and then continue to a gate. Keep forward, passing along the right edge of the conifer plantation, ford a stream and continue along a clear and obvious path that climbs gently above Clochnant. Ahead is an impressive view looking towards the head of the valley and the Berwyn ridge. At a fork take the right-hand, lower path, ford a tributary stream and continue uphill. The path briefly becomes boggy again and this is quite a tiring part of the walk, but you eventually reach a gate at the top of the pass, Bwlch Maen Gwynedd, 2,342 feet (714m) high **C**.

Go through and keep ahead a few yards to enjoy a magnificent view: to the right along the Berwyn ridge to Cadair Berwyn, to the left along the ridge to Cadair Bronwen, behind to the Dee valley, and ahead along the steep-sided, sweeping, curving valley of Cwm Maen Gwynedd. From the bwlch, a path follows a fenceline north to the summit of Cadair Bronwen, the highest point of which is marked by a large cairn – this is one of the legendary sites of King Arthur's Round Table. From the summit it is possible to descend, north-west, beside a fence and through heather to intercept the return route, but this can be uncomfortable for some. The easier option is to retreat to Bwlch Maen Gwynedd, and head back onto the route of ascent, but only for about 100 yards to a fork – probably not noticed on the way up – and take the right-hand path which can be seen heading up over the slopes in front. The path descends initially, then continues gently up, later bearing right and curving left above the head of Blaen Trawsnant. From here there is a superb view to the left of Cadair Berwyn. Continue gently up over Moel Pearce along what has become an undulating track, joining and keeping by a fence on the right, and on arriving at two gates, go through the right-hand one. The track gradually bends right, away from the fence. Go through a gate, beyond which the track braids; your target is the plantation of fir trees ahead. Two gates take you alongside the left edge of these. After the second one, look to your right to spot a stone circle on a low hilltop. It's well worth climbing up to this to enjoy the impressive views and the excellent condition of this evocative Bronze Age monument on Moel Ty-uchaf. From here, head back down a sheep track to regain the fieldside track and walk to a corner and two gates. Use the right-hand one, walking beside a wall on your left through to several gates at a crossing of paths and tracks **D**.

The track ahead becomes tarred beyond a gate. You do not want this one, however. Instead, take the wide gate on your left and join a field road bordered by widely spaced fences and walls. Simply remain on this, going through several bridlegates and across a couple of shallow fords above woodland. At a junction fork right, downhill along a stonier track. Pass

through another gate to reach a junction near a farmhouse. Keep ahead here, passing above the house on a wide path beside a wall and within the edge

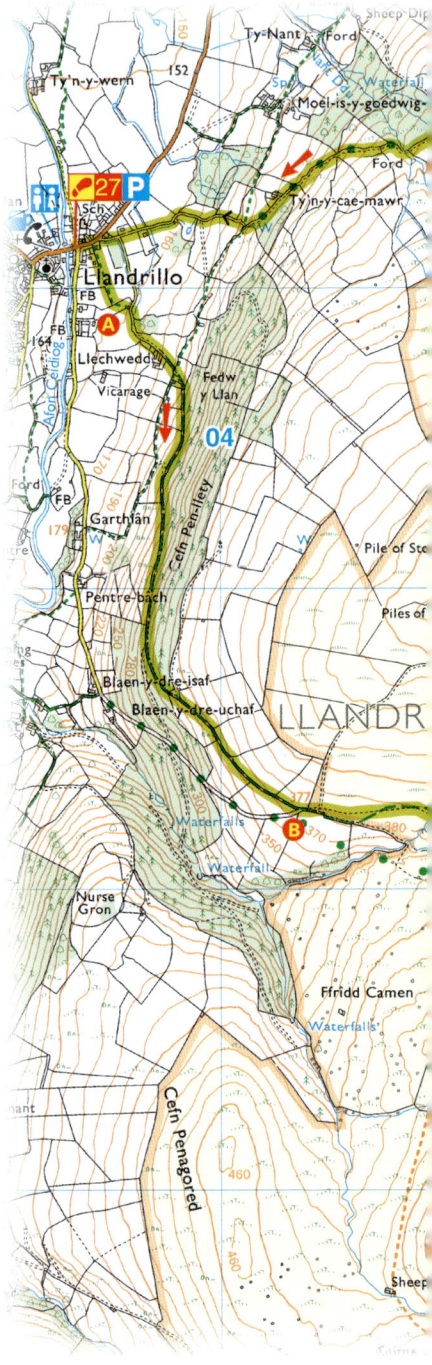

of oak woods. A final gate leads to the top of a steep tarred lane; following this brings you back to Llandrillo's war memorial near the village hall.

walk 28

Moel Sych and Cadair Berwyn

Start
Milltir Cerrig, Denbighshire

Distance
8½ miles (13.5km)

Height gain
1,295 feet (395m)

Approximate time
5 hours

Route terrain
Heather moorland with boardwalks, open mountain summits

Parking
Car park at start, off B4391, north of Llangynog

OS maps
Landranger 125 (Y Bala & Lake Vyrnwy/Llyn Efyrnwy), Explorer 255 (Llangollen & Berwyn)

GPS waypoints
- SJ 017 305
- Ⓐ SJ 029 302
- Ⓑ SJ 042 309
- Ⓒ SJ 072 327

A considerable saving in height gain is the benefit of starting from high on the B4391 Llangynog to Bala road, close by the county boundary. The two targeted summits are given equal height on current OS mapping, and in virtually all contemporary records. *The Summits of Snowdonia*, published in 1984, however, was based on detailed surveyors' records in the archive of Ordnance Survey, and these showed that Moel Sych – the Dry Hill – was one foot higher than Cadair Berwyn. Today, Berwyn gets the bragging rights because of its name. Combined, they are a splendid outing, and access from the west is by a long heathery arm with several intermediate summits to contend with.

The view northwards from the summit of Moel Sych

Both Moel Sych and Cadair Berwyn sit on the boundary between Denbighshire and Powys, the route switching between the two at times but rarely following the concessionary footpath shown on maps. Instead, for much of its length, the route follows a clear path through grouse-hosting heather and for many sections uses boardwalks, which are a blessing if tackling the walk after wet weather.

The first objective is to find the starting path. The parking area adjoins a small disused quarry and from its highest point a couple of peaty paths can be picked out running south-east through heather, and these both lead on to intercept a gravel track, close by an information panel about the 19,770-acre (8,000-hectate) Berwyn National Nature Reserve.

From here, a clear path/boardwalk rises steadily through the area known as Llechwedd Groes, finally passing a slender cairn on Craig Wen **A**. The next objective is a sizeable shelter-cairn **B**, at an elevation of 2,198 feet (670m), with a good view forward of the remaining slopes up onto Moel Sych. The summit lies at the triple historic county boundary point of Montgomeryshire, Denbighshire and Merionethshire, the highest point (historic county top) of Montgomeryshire.

Continue following the boardwalk path and then strike uphill for Ceulan Myheryn before making the final assault on Moel Sych, its summit marked

by a large pile of stones (SJ 066 318).

To the east, the ground drops steeply to Llyn Lluncaws, and this steep escarpment is a feature of the ongoing trek to Cadair Berwyn, which is otherwise straightforward. On the way, however, a small hump (SJ 071 323) is shown to have a height in excess of 2,722 feet (830m, and surveyed at 832m). So, technically, this is the highest point of the Berwyn ridge. The view from Cadair Berwyn **C** is extensive and includes Snowdon (Yr Wyddfa), Cadair Idris, the Rhinogs, Brecon Beacons, Shropshire Hills, the Peak District, Yorkshire Dales, Lake District and the Isle of Man.

From Cadair Berwyn (whichever summit you choose), the retreat to Milltir Cerrig is by the outward route,

Cadair Berwyn

Cadair Berwyn lies between Moel Sych and Cadair Bronwen (Walk 27), and as if to compensate for being trapped between these heathery hills is the only height flanked north and south by a line of steep cliffs. On 23 January 1974 lights and noises were observed on Cadair Berwyn and Cadair Bronwen that were alleged to be related to a UFO sighting. Scientific evidence, however, indicated that the event was generated by an earthquake combined with sightings of a bright meteor widely observed over Wales and northern England at the time.

and almost certainly likely to feel longer than it is.

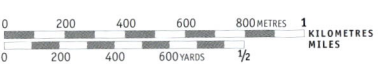

SCALE 1:25000 or 2½ INCHES to 1 MILE 4CM to 1KM

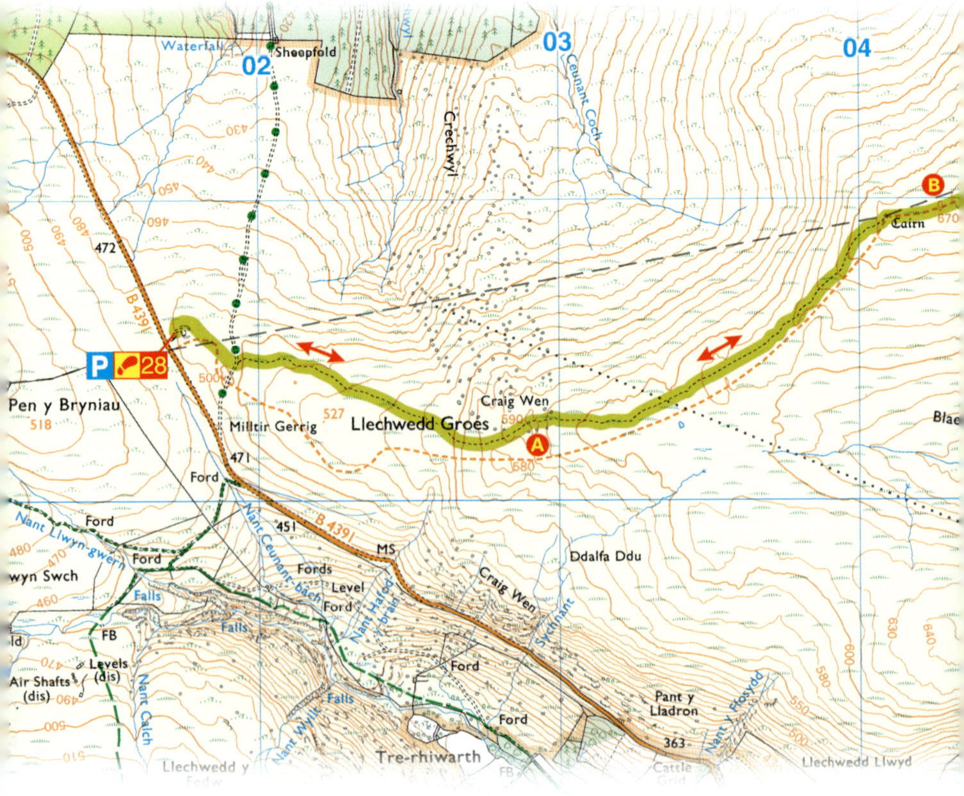

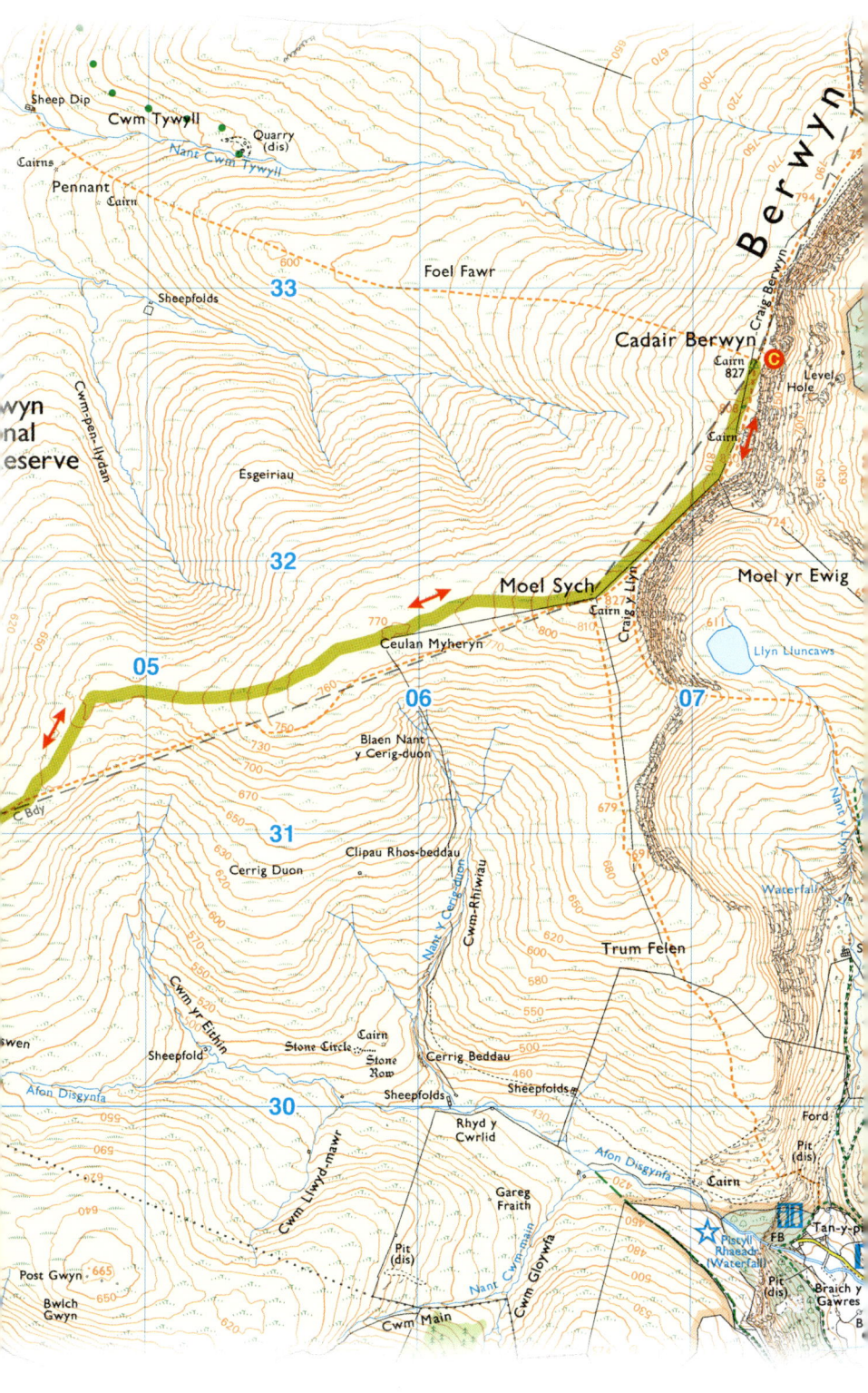

Further Information

 ## Safety on the Hills

The hills, mountains and moorlands of Britain, though of modest height compared with those in many other countries, need to be treated with respect. Friendly and inviting in good weather, they can quickly be transformed into wet, misty, windswept and potentially dangerous areas of wilderness in bad weather. Even on an outwardly fine and settled summer day, conditions can rapidly deteriorate at high altitudes and, in winter, even more so.

Therefore it is advisable always to take both warm and waterproof clothing, sufficient nourishing food, a hot drink, first-aid kit, torch and whistle. Wear suitable footwear, such as strong walking boots or shoes that give a good grip over rocky terrain and on slippery slopes. Try to obtain a local weather forecast and bear it in mind before you start. Do not be afraid to abandon your proposed route and return to your starting point in the event of a sudden and unexpected deterioration in the weather. Do not go alone and allow enough time to finish the walk well before nightfall.

Most of the walks described in this book do not venture into remote wilderness areas and will be safe to do, given due care and respect, at any time of year in all but the most unreasonable weather. Indeed, a crisp, fine winter day often provides perfect walking conditions, with firm ground underfoot and a clarity that is not possible to achieve in the other seasons of the year. A few walks, however, are suitable only for reasonably fit and experienced hill walkers able to use a compass and should definitely not be tackled by anyone else during the winter months or in bad weather, especially high winds and mist. These are indicated in the general description that precedes each of the walks.

 ## Walkers and the Law

The Countryside and Rights of Way Act (CRoW Act 2000) gives a public right of access in England and Wales to land mapped as open country (mountain, moor, heath and down) or registered common land. These areas are known as *open access land*, and include land around the coastline, known as *coastal margin*.

Where You Can Go
Rights of Way
Prior to the introduction of the CRoW Act, walkers could only legally access the countryside along public rights of way. These are either 'footpaths' (for walkers only) or 'bridleways' (for walkers, riders on horseback and pedal cyclists). A third category called 'Byways open to all traffic' (BOATs), is used by motorised vehicles as well as those using non-mechanised transport. Mainly they are green lanes, farm and estate roads, although occasionally they will be found crossing mountainous area.

Rights of way are marked on Ordnance Survey maps. Look for the green broken lines on the Explorer maps, or the red dashed lines on Landranger maps.

The term 'right of way' means exactly what it says. It gives a right of passage over what, for the most part, is private land. Under pre-CRoW legislation walkers were required to keep to the line of the right of way and not stray onto land on either side. If you did inadvertently wander off the right of way, either because of faulty map reading or because the route was not clearly indicated on the ground, you were technically trespassing.

Local authorities have a legal obligation to ensure that rights of way are kept clear and free of obstruction, and are signposted where they leave metalled roads. The duty of local authorities to install signposts extends to the placing of signs along a path or way, but only where the authority considers it necessary to have a signpost or waymark to assist persons unfamiliar with the locality.

CRoW Access Rights
Access Land
As well as being able to walk on existing rights of way, under CRoW legislation you have access to large areas of open land and, under further legislation, a right of coastal access, which is being implemented by Natural England, giving for the first time the right of access around all England's open coast. This includes plans for an England Coast Path (ECP) which will run for 2,795 miles (4,500 kilometres). A corresponding Wales Coast Path has been open since 2012.

Coastal access rights apply within the coastal margin (including along the ECP) unless the land falls into a category of excepted land or is subject to local restrictions, exclusions or diversions.

You can of course continue to use rights of way to cross access land, but you can lawfully leave the path and wander at will in these designated areas.

Where to Walk
Access Land is shown on Ordnance Survey Explorer maps by a light yellow tint surrounded by a pale orange border. New orange coloured 'i' symbols on the maps will show the location of permanent access information boards installed by the access authorities. Coastal Margin is shown on Ordnance Survey Explorer maps by a pink tint.

Restrictions
The right to walk on access land may lawfully be restricted by landowners, but whatever restrictions are put into place on access land they have no effect on existing rights of way, and you can continue to walk on them.

Dogs
Dogs can be taken on access land, but must be kept on leads of two metres or less between 1 March and 31 July, and at all times where they are near livestock. In addition landowners may impose a ban on all dogs from fields where lambing takes place for up to six weeks in any year. Dogs may be banned from moorland used for grouse shooting and breeding for up to five years.

General Obstructions
Obstructions can sometimes cause a problem on a walk and the most common of these is where the path across a field has been ploughed over. It is legal for a farmer to plough up a path provided that it is restored within two weeks. This does not always happen and you are faced with the dilemma of following the line of the path, even if this means treading on crops, or walking round the edge of the field. Although the latter course of action seems the most sensible, it does mean that you would be trespassing.

Other obstructions can vary from overhanging vegetation to wire fences across the path, locked gates or even a cattle feeder on the path.

Use common sense. If you can get round the obstruction without causing damage, do so. Otherwise only remove as much of the obstruction as is necessary to secure passage.

If the right of way is blocked and cannot be followed, there is a long-standing view that in such circumstances there is a right to deviate, but this cannot wholly be relied on. Although it is accepted in law that highways (and that includes rights of way) are for the public service, and if the usual track is impassable, it is for the general good that people should be entitled to pass into another line. However, this should not be taken as indicating a right to deviate whenever a way is impassable. If in doubt, retreat.

Report obstructions to the local authority and/or the Ramblers.

Useful Organisations

CADW: Welsh Government
Ty'r Afon, Bedwas Road
Caerphilly CF83 8WT
Tel: 0300 0256000
https://cadw.gov.wales

Campaign for the Protection
of Rural Wales
Ty Gwyn, 31 High Street, Welshpool,
Powys SY21 7YD
Tel. 01938 552525
www.cprw.org.uk

Long Distance Walkers' Association
www.ldwa.org.uk

National Trust (Wales Regional Office)
Priest House, Tredegar House
Newport NP10 8YW
01633 811659
www.nationaltrust.org.uk

Natural Resources Wales
Tel. 0300 065 3000
Bangor Office
Maes y Ffynnon,
Penrhosgarnedd,
Bangor, LL57 2DW
Dolgellau Office
Government Buildings, Arran Road,
Dolgellau, LL40 1LW
https://naturalresources.wales

Ordnance Survey
www.ordnancesurvey.co.uk

Ramblers Cymru
3 Coopers Yard,
Curran Road,
Cardiff CF10 5NB
Tel. 020 3961 3310
www.ramblers.org.uk/wales

Tourist Information
Visit North Wales
https://visitnorthwales.co.uk
Tourist Information Centres
Conwy: 01492 577566
Llangollen: 01978 860828
Rhyl: 01745 355068

Youth Hostels Association
Trevelyan House,
Dimple Road, Matlock,
Derbyshire DE4 3YH
Tel. 01629 592700
www.yha.org.uk

Ordnance Survey maps for Dee Valley, Clwydian Hills and North East Wales

North East Wales is covered by Ordnance Survey 1:50 000 (1¼ inches to 1 mile or 2cm to 1km) scale Landranger map sheets 115, 116, 117 and 125. These all-purpose maps are packed with information to help you explore the area and show viewpoints, picnic sites, places of interest and caravan and camping sites.

To examine the area in more detail, and especially if you are planning walks, Ordnance Survey Explorer maps at 1:25 000 (2½ inches to 1 mile or 4cm to 1km) scale are ideal:

240 (Oswestry/Croesoswallt)
255 (Llangollen & Berwyn)
256 (Wrexham/Wrecsam & Llangollen)
264 (Vale of Clwyd/Dyffryn Clwyd)
265 (Clwydian Range/Bryniau Clwyd)
266 (Wirral & Chester)

Text:	Terry Marsh. Some walks reused from PF (32) North Wales and Snowdonia, now superseded
Photography:	Terry Marsh, Jonathan Young, Martin Husband, and p66 Dave Newbould, and p70 Henrykc/Shutterstock
Editorial:	Ark Creative (UK) Ltd
Design:	Ark Creative (UK) Ltd

© Crown copyright / Ordnance Survey Limited, 2022
Published by Trotman Publishing Ltd under licence from Ordnance Survey Limited.
Pathfinder, Ordnance Survey, OS and the OS logos are registered trademarks of Ordnance Survey Limited and are used under licence from Ordnance Survey Limited.
Text © Trotman Publishing Limited, 2022

This product includes mapping data licensed from Ordnance Survey
© Crown copyright and database rights (2022) OS 150002047

ISBN: 978-0-31909-202-6

While every care has been taken to ensure the accuracy of the route directions, the publishers cannot accept responsibility for errors or omissions, or for changes in details given. The countryside is not static: hedges and fences can be removed, field boundaries can alter, stiles can be replaced by gates, footpaths can be rerouted and changes in ownership can result in the closure or diversion of some concessionary paths. Also, paths that are easy and pleasant for walking in fine conditions may become slippery, muddy and difficult in wet weather, while stepping stones across rivers and streams may become impassable.

If you find an inaccuracy in either the text or maps, please contact Trotman Publishing at the address below.

First published 2022 by Trotman Publishing.

Trotman Publishing, 19-21D Charles Street, Bath, BA1 1HX
www.pathfinderwalks.co.uk

Printed in India by Replika Press Pvt. Ltd. 1/22

All rights reserved. No part of this publication may be reproduced, transmitted in any form or by any means, or stored in a retrieval system without either the prior written permission of the publisher, or in the case of reprographic reproduction a licence issued in accordance with the terms and licences issued by the CLA Ltd.

A catalogue record for this book is available from the British Library.

Front cover: *The Beginning and the End,* Prestatyn
Page 1: Heading for Cyrn-y-brain

 **Britain's best-loved walking guides**

Scotland
Pathfinder Walks
3 ISLE OF SKYE
4 CAIRNGORMS
7 FORT WILLIAM & GLEN COE
19 DUMFRIES & GALLOWAY
23 LOCH LOMOND, THE TROSSACHS, & STIRLING
27 PERTHSHIRE, ANGUS & FIFE
30 LOCH NESS & INVERNESS
31 OBAN, MULL & KINTYRE
46 ABERDEEN & ROYAL DEESIDE
47 EDINBURGH, PENTLANDS & LOTHIANS
82 ORKNEY & SHETLAND
83 NORTH COAST 500 & NORTHERN HIGHLANDS

North of England
Pathfinder Walks
15 YORKSHIRE DALES
22 MORE LAKE DISTRICT
28 NORTH YORK MOORS
35 NORTHUMBERLAND & SCOTTISH BORDERS
39 DURHAM, NORTH PENNINES & TYNE AND WEAR
42 CHESHIRE
49 VALE OF YORK & YORKSHIRE WOLDS
53 LANCASHIRE
60 LAKE DISTRICT
63 PEAK DISTRICT
64 SOUTH PENNINES
71 THE HIGH FELLS OF LAKELAND
73 MORE PEAK DISTRICT

Short Walks
1 YORKSHIRE DALES
2 PEAK DISTRICT
3 LAKE DISTRICT
13 NORTH YORK MOORS

Wales
Pathfinder Walks
10 SNOWDONIA
18 BRECON BEACONS
34 PEMBROKESHIRE & CARMARTHENSHIRE
41 MID WALES
55 GOWER, SWANSEA & CARDIFF
78 ANGLESEY, LLEYN & SNOWDONIA
79 DEE VALLEY, CLWYDIAN HILLS & NORTH EAST WALES

Short Walks
14 SNOWDONIA
31 BRECON BEACONS

Heart of England
Pathfinder Walks
6 COTSWOLDS
20 SHERWOOD FOREST & THE EAST MIDLANDS
29 WYE VALLEY & FOREST OF DEAN
74 THE MALVERNS TO WARWICKSHIRE
80 SHROPSHIRE
81 STAFFORDSHIRE
84 BERKSHIRE, BUCKINGHAMSHIRE & OXFORDSHIRE

Short Walks
4 COTSWOLDS
32 HEREFORDSHIRE & THE WYE VALLEY

East of England
Pathfinder Walks
44 ESSEX
45 NORFOLK
48 SUFFOLK
50 LINCOLNSHIRE & THE WOLDS
51 CAMBRIDGESHIRE & THE FENS

South West of England
Pathfinder Walks
1 SOUTH DEVON & DARTMOOR
5 CORNWALL
9 EXMOOR & THE QUANTOCKS
11 DORSET & THE JURASSIC COAST
26 DARTMOOR
68 NORTH & MID DEVON
69 SOUTH WEST ENGLAND'S COAST
76 SOMERSET & THE MENDIPS
77 WILTSHIRE

Short Walks
8 DARTMOOR
9 CORNWALL
21 EXMOOR
29 SOUTH DEVON

South East of England
Pathfinder Walks
8 KENT
12 NEW FOREST, HAMPSHIRE & SOUTH DOWNS
25 THAMES VALLEY & CHILTERNS
54 HERTFORDSHIRE & BEDFORDSHIRE
65 SURREY
66 SOUTH DOWNS NATIONAL PARK & WEST SUSSEX
67 SOUTH DOWNS NATIONAL PARK & EAST SUSSEX
72 THE HOME COUNTIES FROM LONDON BY TRAIN

Short Walks
23 NEW FOREST NATIONAL PARK
27 ISLE OF WIGHT

Practical Guide
75 NAVIGATION SKILLS FOR WALKERS

City Walks
LONDON
OXFORD
EDINBURGH